GAME
GET SOME!

To
Dernardo !
Be + Some !
(Love) Ken

KENYA MOORE

GAME GET SOME!
WHAT WOMEN REALLY WANT

DARK HORSE
PRODUCTIONS

Published by Dark Horse Productions, LLC

Dark Horse Productions, LLC registered offices are at:
264 S. LaCienega Blvd. Ste 577
Beverly Hills, CA 90211
DARKHORSEPRODLLC.COM

First Printing, November 2007
10 9 8 7 6 5 4 3 2 1

ISBN-13   978-0-9797675-0-0
ISBN-10   0-9797675-0-4

Printed in the United States of America
Cover designed by R4Media
Photographer: Leslie Bohm
Make Up: Suzie Kim
Hair: Ebony Thomas
Illustrations: Tony Ortiz

This book is dedicated to all my beautiful brothers who exclusively love women. Mwah! I love you back.

THE PLAYBOOK

Acknowledgements

I've been truly blessed in my life and I have to thank God for always having His Angel on my shoulder at all times.

I wholeheartedly thank all of my loyal fans who have hung in there with me throughout my career. Thank you for keeping me 'gassed up' and motivating me to keep going. I thank all my family: the Moores and the Grants—for loving me and occasionally for tolerating me ☺. A special thanks to my Aunt Lisa Duncan for always "fixing it." To my grandmother Doris, who taught me that I was "the prize" and a big thank you to my cousin Tamica AKA "mini me" for always looking out for her baby sis. To my "bestest" girlfriends Lauren, Chanda, and Camille, you are my sisters, now and forever. And to TyTy: the baby sis I always wanted, whether lost or found, you never leave my heart. I'm so proud of you! To my glam squad: Linda Stokes, Tanya Stine and Suzie Kim for always hooking me up and creating the smoke and mirrors. To Jeff Stetson, for being the talented, supportive, and incredible man that you are—not to mention a brilliant writer—thank you for your invaluable direction and guidance throughout my blossoming writing career, and for being a true friend.

I'd like to extend a special thank you to the incredible women who have modeled and exemplified elegance, class, sophistication, unfaltering self-worth, and dignity for me both up close and from afar: my Aunt Lori Smyth, adopted Aunt Lisa Phillips, my friends Ms. Roberta Shields, Ms. Jackie Mobley, Wanda Fisher, and my role models, Vanessa Williams, Maya Angelou, Oprah Winfrey, and Angela Bassett. If I have just a fraction of your inner beauty and strength, then I am well on my way to being the woman I strive to be.

Finally, to the few men I have loved and cared for: thank you for teaching me about my shortcomings, my strengths, and about myself. Thank you for helping me to know how to distinguish the "keepers" that make the team, from the "throwbacks" who get cut.

To EG, a definite a keeper and an inspiration for this book: You are a rare kind, and all men should be like you, I love you.

And a special thank you to CRM, for being my "Mr. Big" and making me know how deeply, how completely, and how absolutely unconditionally I can love a man. And thank you for allowing me to experience the wondrous and pure love of your little one (the "baby love" of my life) whom I love like my own. And lastly, thank you for breaking my heart into a million and two pieces. But it is with these two pieces that I have been able to fuse back together (thankfully), to make myself whole again, which in time, will allow me to open up my heart to "the one."

-Kenya

Game- any activity that involves intense interest and competitiveness and is carried out by its own specific and often unspoken rules.

<u>Introduction</u>

Caution: This book is not meant for losers, or for guys who can't get a date of the two-legged variety. It's meant to be used as reference tool to help you *polish* your game. Or more simply, it's an entertaining and insightful dating "rules of engagement" guide. No one man can know everything there is to know about women. But with my help, you will come very close!

Forget what you've been told. ANY MAN CAN GET ANY GIRL. I can prove it. Have you ever seen a dyme with an average looking or even *below* average looking guy? The leggy model with a Joe Schmoe? The beautiful celebrity with a far less than beautiful celebrity man, who as a couple, fuels message boards, gossip rags, and water cooler conversations all asking the question: How did he get *her?* I bet you have, and I bet you've also wondered: "If he did it, why can't I?"

Perhaps the girl of your dreams seems unattainable because you have made her unattainable in your mind. Most men assume that their "dream girl"—the beautiful woman, the high-profile celebrity, or the powerful businesswoman—only dates or hooks up with the rich guy or the bad boy with incredible sexual prowess. Not true.

The truth is, whether she's a grocery store clerk, the Secretary of State, or a CEO of a multi-billion dollar company, ALL women have the same basic needs. If therefore, you can tap into what her individual needs and desires are, you can win her affection...and you don't have to be a Rock Star or a Baller to do it!

Still, most men have *no clue* as to how to pull the woman they see everyday, or secretly wish to date, but just can't bring themselves to even speak to.

You may ask yourself, 'Why should I take advice from a single, successful, independent, former beauty queen, slightly over 30 who has never been married?' Answer? Exactly because I *am* a single, successful, independent, former beauty queen, slightly over 30, who has never been married! In other words (hint, hint!), there's a *reason* why I'm still single. By now, I know **exactly** what men are doing wrong.

And NO, I'm not a lesbian, or interested in the ménage à trois thing. I absolutely love, love, *love* men and I have many girlfriends who adore men just as I do. They are young, successful, independent, attractive, and looking for love. But they can't seem to find the right fit. So in essence, that means that there is an entire *world* of amazing women for your taking. You just need an honest, unbiased, straight-forward female's perspective to show you the way. **HELP ME HELP YOU!**

From time to time, just so you're aware, I will make generalizations about each sex. These broad strokes are based upon many things: some polling, data collection, research studies as well as human experience and good ol' common sense. The point is, our conclusive evidence boils down to this: **ALL MEN ARE DOGS!** LOL. Just joking. I wanted to make sure you're still paying attention.

CHAPTER ONE

THE TROPHY

Relationships are like chess games, you must play to win from the very first move and calculate every single move 10 moves in advance. How ironic is the fact that the Queen is the most valuable piece on the board? And that is your mission: to put the woman you desire in a checkmate position where she has to surrender or be taken.

This should be obvious, but just in case it is not, **all women are NOT created equal.** Aside from the physical aspects of a woman—whether she has long legs, rounded hips, pixie hair, mocha skin, hazel eyes, or saliva-worthy toes—each woman has her own unique *internal* features. People believe that women were put here to be companions, who would form equal, fulfilling unions with men. Whether you believe in God or not is not the question; men and women are naturally and physically made for each other. This is the natural order of things on

Planet Puddin' (PUDDINGTHEMOVIE.COM in theaters next year). Shameless plug, I know, but it works for me! I should say here that I have nothing against same-sex unions, but I can only speak from my perspective and personal experience. So, sorry boys, and some of you girls—I felt the wave of disappointment from you.

WHY MEN LOVE WOMEN

Girls, girls, girls! Who knows what first made men love women? Maybe it was the little girl who sat in front of you in elementary school with the pigtails you pulled. Perhaps it was your next-door neighbor, the one you played doctor with in the basement of your home. Or perhaps you were a player-in-the-making early on, setting your sights on your voluptuous sixth-grade teacher. You know, the one who gave you an unwelcome boner in class, prompting you to carry extra books to hide your excitement and embarrassment. Maybe it was the first sign of your young female classmate's hips beginning to widen, as you mischievously eyed her nipples as they peeked underneath her softly colored pink cotton t-shirt. Maybe it was the sweet glances stolen in homeroom that drove you crazy enough to scribble that first girl's name in your notebooks and daydream about her all day. Or, was it when your older brother showed you his personal stash of Playboy magazines, where your eyes first feasted on a nappy dugout, or imagined your hands probing the model's prominent breasts that first got you all shook up? Whatever they were, those indelible images were long-lasting and irreversible. Bottom line, you were hooked on women from day one, and there is no turning back now!

YOUR FIRST LOVE

Most little boys grow to love and cherish their mothers more than anything in the world. She was your first example of love. She was there when you needed to be held. She was there to show you affection when daddy scolded you. She was there for you. She was patient and kind, and told you how smart you were. Your mother was there for you and still loved you when you misbehaved in school. She was there to remind you to focus on your studies, and warn you about staying away from "fast" little girls. Most likely, your mother is the first woman you ever fell in love with. Not in a physical way of course, but in an emotional sense. She was your model of love. Through her actions, she taught you how to care, how to receive love, and how to love others. It was the way she looked at you when you walked into the room. Perhaps you were the light of her life and you felt that as a child, even when she would scream at you to pick your clothes up off the floor. You knew you were loved, and that love, came from a **woman**.

So why am I talking about your mother? Because so many men often will unconsciously fall in love with a woman who is like his mother, because again, his mother is the ultimate love of his life. Mothers naturally sacrifice and do anything to make their children happy in order to show their children they are loved. As a result, it is sometimes a woman's inclination to treat a man like a child. But normally, a woman most desires a man who can protect *her*, nurture *her*, and make *her* feel cherished and

3

safe. And fortunately, most men *have* had a good and healthy, nurturing "first love" with their mothers. So as your little peckers grew in size, men, so did your natural thirst and desire to seek out women who would love and adore you as your mother did. Physiological changes and hormones only heightened a maturing boy's natural instinct to hunt for and "conquer" this thing called *woman.*

Men love being the knight in shining armor. They love the way a woman needs them, because they have a need to be needed. Men also have a need to be respected, and have an ingrained need to be successful.

Only a woman can make a man feel all these things and more. She can comfort him with her soft words, spoken from her even softer lips. She can be a sweet, supple place for him to fall into when the world beats him down. She can let a man nestle into her curves, making him feel comforted and at home. And last but not least, when you're in need of a release, men, she can back that thang up and make you scream like a banshee! After all, we all know what rules the world— and it ain't money!

CHAPTER 2

BOYS -VS- GIRLS

Boys and girls, or rather men and women, are inherently different. This is the foundational understanding needed to move forward and comprehend the subsequent chapters. Men and women communicate, relate, and speak to each other *differently*.

Understanding these basic dissimilarities will allow you to communicate with women on a more effective level. If you can master this art form, your girl will feel as though she is talking to one of her girlfriends when speaking with you, thereby allowing you to get closer to her faster. Having this understanding offers you invaluable tools when it comes to communicating with anyone, on any level, whether it is your boss, a co-worker, or your mother. But *especially* if it's a female on the other end of the telephone line whom you wish to know better, or possibly resolve an issue with.

By understanding women on a more profound level, many things will make better sense to you. You will also have a heightened sense of how to effectively communicate with people, in general. Men frequently commit the crime of thinking that *women* think and communicate and respond to situations the same way they do. This could not be further from the truth. Organically—we are poles apart. That is what makes a woman a woman and a man a man. Because of these natural differences, unsurprisingly, conflicts arise.

I became more acutely aware of this truth as an actor in a classroom setting. There, it was amazing to me to see how people could be listening to the same thing, yet hear it so differently. We all can hear the exact same phrase, yet process it differently in our heads. And the biggest crime we can commit is to respond to *our* "interpretation" of the question, issue, or comment coming from the opposite sex, rather, from *their* interpretation. Men and women both are guilty of this, but I have to say that *men* are the most frequent offenders.

WOMEN LOVE TO TALK

If you have ever dated a woman, then you realize women love to talk. This is because communication is of utmost importance to us! Talking, relating, and sharing with people generates harmony and fulfillment in our lives. A woman's sense of self is defined by her feelings, and by the quality—not the quantity—of her relationships. And we can all agree that happiness is defined by the individual's own sense of fulfillment. But this is key to understanding a woman. If she never becomes a powerful media mogul, or the head of Doctors Without Borders, or the great fashion designer she dreamed of being when she was a little girl, she can be happy if she has fulfilling and loving relationships.

WHY WOMEN LOVE TO TALK

Women feel a release when they talk about their problems. Women talk to exchange, convey, and/or compile information with one another. Women also tend to verbalize their thoughts, and often use their listener as a sounding board. When it comes to her troubles, as she speaks, there's something about hearing herself articulate her woes that allows her intuition to flow, which in turn helps her find the answers she needs. Afterwards, she feels better. Talking and sharing is a release for her. Another reason she shares her feelings is to create relational bonds and to establish and maintain intimacy.

For the woman, cultivating a relationship happens through communication, talking and sharing. Nevertheless, if you want even the slightest chance of getting close to a woman, you must learn how to communicate *like* a woman. An Oldhead once said, "**You must become one with the pussy**." In general, men do not like to sit for hours, discussing their feelings, or what they saw at the mall that day, or whether Angelina Jolie stole Brad Pitt from Jennifer Aniston. I'm not implying that "trifling" topics are the only things women discuss with each other. My point is, girls have a natural flow to our multifaceted conversations. Herein lies the Number One "natural conflict" between men and women, too. If you are trying to win a woman's heart, you must do the following:

MEN MUST LEARN TO LISTEN

This is the Number One complaint women have about men: **"men don't listen."** Unfortunately, finding a man who listens is like striking oil. And we all know how expensive gas is these days!

Communication is easy when a man "gets" what his woman is saying—when he correctly interprets the information she is trying to convey. This is not an easy task, but requires dedication and a desire to understand women. It also requires a great deal of practice. But by learning how to correctly interpret what a woman is really saying, you will understand her. You will understand how to relate to her. You will understand how to get closer to her. And, you'll be able to anticipate her needs and desires, enabling you to *fulfill* those needs and desires.

The Art of Listening

A man should listen without judging or without feeling blamed or responsible for what she is saying. Just actively listen! I'm not suggesting that you need to spend hours at a time on the phone with her, but keep in mind that the longer you spend talking to your girl about the things that are important to her, the more you create an intimate bond. Wanting to learn about her should come naturally to you if you are genuinely interested in her. By doing this, she will begin to feel the connection between the two of you. She will brag to all of her girlfriends about how well you express yourself. She will tell them that you are nothing like other guys. In these occasional extended conversations with your lady, the goal is to ask her about herself. Get to know how she thinks. Learn about the woman she is, the woman she wants to become.

The following questions are meant to be mere examples to guide you in getting to know the woman you desire better. Now mind you, these questions should not be asked as though you are reading a laundry-list. Rather, they should flow naturally during your conversations. When a man takes the time to ask us about ourselves, we feel a chemical reaction take place within us. Our body temperature rises, and our endorphins kick into high gear. All this activity makes us feel euphoric and content. So, ask her a million questions. I'll give you the first seventy-five:

THE FIRST 75 QUESTIONS TO ASK A WOMAN

ABOUT HER PERSONALITY

1. What is she most afraid of?
2. Who are her best friends?
3. What would each of them say about her?
4. What can she tell you about herself that no one knows?
5. What is her philosophy on life?
6. Was she a tomboy or a prissy girl?
7. Is she a leader or a follower?
8. If she could live any place where would it be?
9. If she could visit/travel to any place where would it be?
10. Who does she have a girl crush on?
11. When was the first time she ever got inebriated?
12. Where was it?

13. What is her most embarrassing moment?
14. What is her favorite movie?
15. What actress would she like to play her in her life story?
16. What historical person would she want to meet man or a woman?
17. Thongs or boy shorts?
18. Who was her high school crush?
19. Who taught her how to ride a bike?
20. Did she ever wear braces?
21. Who was her idol growing up?
22. What is her Achilles' heel?
23. Least favorite body part on a man?
24. Least favorite body part on herself?
25. Does she have any phobias?
26. What wild animal would she want to have as a pet?
27. Is she domesticated?
28. What is her best talent?
29. Has she ever competed in a beauty pageant?
30. What does she consider to be her personality flaws?
31. What does she think about cosmetic surgery?
32. What is the most daring thing she has ever done?
33. Does she have a MySpace page?
34. What would be her idea of a perfect day/date?
35. Michael Jackson or Prince?
36. Vanity or Apollonia?
37. Mary Ann or Ginger?
38. Who was the first Singer/Artist whose poster she put on her wall?
39. What movie makes her cry every time she sees it?
40. Hillary or Barack?

ABOUT SEX

41. What celebrity can "get it" with no questions asked?
42. Who was her first boyfriend?
43. Has she seen him since she's grown up?
44. What was her first kiss like?
45. Has she ever been with a virgin?
46. Her favorite body part on a man?
47. If she only had seven minutes for sex would she like it soft and slow or hard and fast?
48. As a joke: How soon can you see her naked?
49. Craziest place she has ever had sex?
50. Craziest place she wants to have sex?

ABOUT HER CAREER

51. Where does she want to be in five years?
52. In ten years?
53. What is her passion in life?
54. What would she be doing if every job paid the same?
55. What are her goals and dreams in life?

ABOUT HER FAMILY

56. What is her family like?
57. Where did she grow up?
58. What was it like in her household?
59. What kind of relationship does she have with her mother?
60. With her father?
61. With her siblings (if any)?

ABOUT HER COLLEGE EXPERIENCE

62. What was/is her major?
63. Why did she choose that particular curriculum or degree?
64. Was/Is she a part of a sorority?
65. Is she still friends with any of them?
66. What's the craziest thing she did while rushing?
67. Does she play any instruments?
68. Ever take a dance class in school?
69. What class did she hate/love?
70. What was/is it like for her in school?
71. Did she have any school recitals or plays?
72. If so, who/what did she play?
73. Was she a bully in school or the nerd who got picked on or the stuck-up cool girl?
74. Did she win any special election at school (i.e. most likely to succeed)?
75. Did she run for or hold an office or committee? Position? Post?

While women do like to be asked about ourselves, there are some questions you should *not* ask!

My personal policy is Don't ask, Don't tell. I do not advise asking a woman any and every thing that comes to mind. But if you want to be hard-headed and risk offending her, or risk her slapping you in the face, or her never speaking to you again, go ahead and ask the following...

PERSONAL QUESTIONS TO **NEVER** ASK A WOMAN:

- How old are you?
- How much do you weigh?

- What size do you wear?
- How many sexual partners have you had?
- Is that your real hair?
- Are those your real eyes or colored contacts?
- Do you have breast implants?
- How much money do you make?
- When was the last time you had sex?
- If she has several children: Do all of your children have the same father?

If you want to compliment her, then do it. Needing to know if something is "real" is irrelevant. On the other hand, some women don't mind revealing their "beauty secrets." They will readily tell you which Korean beauty mart they bought their fake ponytail! Another woman, though, will be embarrassed if you can tell the blonde hair she's wearing she can sit on is fake, or the 48 triple-D breasts that don't move when she is on her back are **not** naturally hers. Better to be safe than sorry! If you are attracted to her, none of this should matter (unless you have an aversion to a particular "enhancement" technique, that is). You will learn in time.

Also, do not debate religion or politics. These are personal issues. The last thing you want to do is get into religious debates. Talk about a no-win situation.

WHEN PROBLEMS ARISE

MOST WOMEN DO NOT SAY WHAT THEY REALLY MEAN

This has got to be one of the most frustrating differences between the sexes for men. It is one of the biggest reasons for conflict between us. Most women do not say what they are actually thinking or feeling. We will go on and on, and argue with you about something totally unrelated to what we are really feeling inside. I'm so sorry that we women have a tendency to drive you guys crazy with this. To be fair, men are guilty of this too, at times, but by far, women are most prone to this type of miscommunication. Women often send the wrong messages by what we say, what we do, show, think, or mean, which can be altogether different. Sometimes, a woman herself doesn't exactly know what she is trying to say!

Many times when a woman is angry or hurt, she may lash out without clearly knowing how to express why she is having the feelings she is, or, how to express to someone how to avoid and/or help her from feeling that way. So often times, you will find yourself in a "dumb" argument where you feel the "crime" does not fit the "punishment." For instance, she's complaining that you bought the wrong dog food. Or that the pink in your tie is not pink, but actually mauve, or some insane argument that makes no sense to you that she "started." This is usually a good indication that she is not expressing what she is really angry about. You must get her to calm down and try to talk.

My suggestion here is simple. Take her by the hands, hold her tightly, sit her down and then look deep into her eyes. After she softens a little, ask these questions: "Why are you really upset? Please calm down and talk to me. Whatever is going on with you, I want to understand. I don't want to make you upset, or contribute to why you are so angry."

You are offering her a sounding board. Women want to talk. So the goal is to get her to talk, and not fight.

MEN HAVE LEARNED TO ADAPT AND EVOLVE

Throughout time, nature has shown us that most creatures successfully learn to adapt to their environment. Men are no different. Therefore, in response to our unique way of communicating, men have adapted their own communicative skills; and one way they do this is by **interpreting** what women say. The reason they do this is in fact quite admirable. Still, herein lies the problem: a man's interpretation of what a woman is saying is usually **incorrect.** From a man's standpoint, the goal is to try to go directly to the problem. He wants to immediately and expeditiously fix what's broken. He wants to find a *solution*.

Example:

A woman comes home angry and spent. She shares with her man how she spent the day arguing with a mechanic over the price of a brake job. Her account of their exchange goes on for more than 15 minutes. His instinct is to ask her if she wants him to pay the difference in price between what the mechanic wants to charge, and what she thinks she should pay to end it all and to do something nice for her. Seems reasonable, right? While this is certainly a nice gesture, the man is missing out on his lady's point entirely, as well as missing out on a great opportunity to bond with her.

Here's what she is saying: "I find it frustrating that, because I am a woman, people constantly try to take advantage of me and make me feel stupid. I am *not* stupid, and it angers me that someone would try to treat me this way. I'm not asking for your help; I just want you to listen."

When a woman shares things, a man may feel are trivial, or even childish, all she wants is someone she can vent to. His ears may start bleeding after the sixth or seventh minute of hearing what he considers "the same thing over and over," but an occasional "umm hmm," or "I understand why that may have frustrated you," or a simple show of support to validate her feelings is all she really needs.

Other Examples of Men's "Misinterpretations":

Example #1
She says:
We never do anything.

He hears:
I'm not happy. I can't believe how boring you are. We never do anything together. You're not sexy, you're not exciting anymore, and you bore me to tears. I'd rather watch paint dry.

What she means is:
I miss you. I miss your company. You are fun to be with. I want to go out somewhere. I want to do something together. I love being with you and I need for you to make some time for me.

Example #2
She says:
You don't love me anymore.

He hears:
You're worthless. You are mean. You are selfish. I have been with you through thick and thin, and this is how you treat me. Why am I still with you? You don't care about anybody but your damn self. Now I'm stuck with you!

What she means is:
I know you love me and I see it in everything you do for me. I had a hard day. I feel like you are acting distant today, which makes me afraid, because I don't want to lose you. I love you. I need you to reassure me that you love me, and that I'm the *only* woman you love.

Example #3
She says:
My feet hurt.

He hears:
A faint Charlie Brown episode in his ear—"Wah, wah, wah!"

What she means is:
Please turn off the Super Bowl and pay attention to me. (Nice try, ladies—we all know that this will never happen!)

THE 'NEVER-DOs' WHEN BEING A GOOD LISTENER

NEVER, EVER INVALIDATE A WOMAN'S FEELINGS

This is a cardinal sin. If you want to get a tongue-lashing, if you want to build up resentment, if you want to foster ill feelings that will threaten your relationship, tell a woman; "you don't make sense" or, "I don't understand why you are so upset." True, our feelings don't always immediately make sense to a man, but, they are **always** valid and require empathy. You don't have to agree with a woman to understand where she is coming from. Just because you don't agree with how a woman feels when she is expressing herself to you or explaining her problems, does not mean she does not have a right to feel the way she feels. You can still be a good listener.

Never say that she is "silly" to feel a certain way. Or ask her *how* she could feel that way or tell her that she is wrong. You will only infuriate her, and confirming for her that you make her feel like you are an insensitive, condescending, clueless idiot for not clearly seeing and understanding why she feels the way she does. Even if you don't agree, she is a human being with sometimes volatile emotions. It is your duty as a friend to only make comments that **validate** her feelings. Instead of apathy or criticism, offer her this instead: "I understand". And, "You have every right to feel that way. I'm sorry this happened to you." Or, "I'm sorry you feel that way." If you have offended her yourself, perhaps you can say, "I'm sorry I made you feel that way; it was not my intention." She will consider you the best thing since sliced bread and think you are a rare breed of man.

DO NOT TRY TO CHANGE HER FEELINGS WHEN SHE IS UPSET

If your woman is upset, just let her talk it out. Do not offer solutions. You might simply ask, "How can I help?"

She will let you know if she wants your help, or she may require it at another time; but primarily, by your generous offer, she will feel that you are there for her in the way she needs you to be and this is the most important point. Your cool points have just skyrocketed!

CHAPTER 3

SPECIAL TEAMS

We are different, men and women, in more ways than just physically. (Although some of you *do* have man-boobs. Ha-Ha!) Our emotional needs vary greatly as significantly as our physiques. Men need a kind of love that is trusting, appreciative, supportive, and accepting, in order to feel *respected.* How many countless Scarface episodes or gangster movies have you seen where a star's ego is blown way out of proportion? When someone makes the unforgivable mistake and "disrespects" him, he's quick to pull out an assault rifle and level it at the nose of his offender! Men don't handle being disrespected very well. This cuts a man to his core. Men will fight total strangers in a club, on a train, or at work, over this single issue. They fight for their honor, and no offense of this kind is ever petty to them.

Our emotional paradigm:

WOMEN NEED TO FEEL
CHERISHED
ADORED
SAFE
SUPPORTED
UNDERSTOOD

MEN NEED TO FEEL
RESPECTED
POWERFUL
ADMIRED
SEXUALLY DESIRED

MEN NEED TO SHOW WOMEN
PATIENCE
UNDERSTANDING
ACCEPTANCE
DEDICATION
STABILITY

WOMEN NEED TO SHOW MEN
FAITH
CONFIDENCE
TRUST
ADMIRATION

MEN'S GREATEST FEARS
Fear of rejection
Fear of failure
Inadequacy
Submission/Loss of Control

WOMEN'S GREATEST FEARS
Fear of not being heard
Fear of not being loved
Fear of not being cherished
Fear of not being valued

MEN'S INSECURITIES IN A RELATIONSHIP

One of man's deepest fears in a relationship is thinking his woman feels that he is not good enough

You must understand yourself in order to know what you may project to women. Fear lies within us all and often handicaps us with the opposite sex.

One of a man's deepest fears when it comes to a woman is that he is not good enough, or that he is incompetent. Men often focus on getting more power, more money, more recognition, and more success. This is why a man is primarily the provider, as evidenced since the beginning of time. Again, this speaks to the natural order of things. I did not make up the rules, but having gained insight into our natural differences, I can completely understand why it works this way. A man needs to feel powerful. He needs to feel successful.

One of man's primary needs is to be respected. He needs to feel like he is king of his castle. He needs to feel like he is running things. That he "pays the cost to be the boss." You often hear a man say, "This is *my* house!" He needs to be in control; be the breadwinner. In our society, people devalue men who ask for spousal support, as evidenced by Jonathan Plummer (Terry McMillan's ex) and others. We do not respect men who cannot take care of themselves. If you understand how women view these scenarios, you will understand what turns her off and/or attracts her to a certain type of man.

DIFFERENCE IN SHOW OF EMOTIONS

The more a man cares, the more his feelings are heightened and exposed. He then tends to pull away, giving less of himself at the first sign of vulnerability. For this type of man, it is his natural instinct to pull away when he feels like he is losing control. A man needs to feel in control of *everything,* including his feelings.

A man's primary need is to be autonomous

Your average man fears the "we," the "our," and the commitment. He doesn't want to have to answer to anyone. In his world he is king: 'I am man, hear me roar.' This is a part of his power. Therefore he feels a woman must *submit to him.* When he senses he is losing control, or the balance of power is shifting, he will shut down.

The autonomous man will pull away as a defense mechanism against losing control of his emotions, or getting too close to someone; he doesn't want to be hurt or to ever be vulnerable. This is his struggle: He does not want to lose control or fly blindly. Men were taught to suppress their emotions. When a man starts to feel emotions on a deeper level, he will instinctively fight and/or take flight. Eat or be eaten. And in an attempt to regain his control, he will overcompensate. He will hide his vulnerability. He will behave selfishly and only think of himself. His attitude will say, "I am an asshole and I won't apologize for it." Sadly, the woman he cares for is his casualty along with the relationship.

To accomplish this pulling away, a man may focus on his work, or even on other women, just to avoid getting "caught up." He is also often ridiculed by his friends for even caring for a woman. To avoid looking like a "punk", he then may exhibit "doggish" behavior toward his woman, just to show to his friends that he is not "catching feelings" for someone and that he is not "weak."

Women, on the other hand, are the opposite. When a woman is in love, she feels compelled to offer her love unconditionally, and without reason. She welcomes these feelings and expresses it through what she does. Love is a source of great fulfillment and happiness to her, knowing she has someone to care for. She is compelled to offer herself without limitation. This brings her happiness. Her nature is to help and to nurture. The greater her love is for someone, the more she is willing to give. Women intuitively sense the needs of others. They see this as an opportunity to show someone how much they care; a woman loves to anticipate what a man requires. Love, to her, is you never having to ask. She instinctively tries to anticipate your needs.

Take for instance a mother toting a diaper bag; she automatically anticipates the needs of her child. This is evidenced by what she packs in the bag: snacks for when the child gets hungry, toys for when he gets antsy and wants to play, water or juice for when he gets thirsty, a sweater, in case the child gets cold, a change of clothes, in case he gets dirty, and diapers, games, wipes—any and everything her child may require. She enjoys and is fulfilled in knowing that she can meet even the smallest need of someone she loves.

WOMEN ARE VERY INTUITIVE

Women have the gift of intuition. A mother has it to the tenth power, but women in general have it in abundance. Their sensitivities hone in to the most minuscule of details and subtlety of nuances—things men will never tap into. A woman can sense the difference in the way a person looks at her man, from one time to the next—especially when it's another woman, and that woman wants to do you. Trust me, your woman will know. We peep the way your posture changes around certain people or if you are wearing new cologne? Did you break a routine in any way? Are you starting to do new things, learning new sports, or dressing differently? Is the sex different? It could be the way you avoid certain people, or issues, or places; these little changes are actually "clues," setting off tiny alarms in our brains. With women, the smallest of details matters the most. Because we are emotionally driven, we have learned to listen to our gut instincts.

WOMEN ARE FAR MORE EMOTIONAL THAN MEN

You must respect a woman's sensitivities. Women are natural nurturers and caretakers. We are raised to be this way. We were encouraged to talk. To be open. To communicate. All our early and rudimentary relationships supported this behavior.

When we fell down and scraped our knees, girls ran to our mothers who encouraged us to cry and to get it out. We learned sensitivity, how to sacrifice and take care of others, because our mothers modeled such behavior. We could talk to her about our feelings and she encouraged us to do so. We could come to her with all of our problems and talk to her about how our day went. Mother explained puberty, menstruation and, hopefully, sex. Because of her, we are sensitive to others, and to how we are perceived by others. We do not like to hurt others, nor do we not like to be hurt. (And when we do purposely offend or hurt someone, we can often dish it out but can't take it!) Mother took care of the house and made sure the family was fed. She made sure we brushed our teeth at night and were presentable at all times. She taught us how to carry ourselves like ladies.

Women are also sensitive to the earth and the world's time clock. Our bodies and our emotions are cyclical: this is clearly evidenced by our menstrual cycles. Our sensitivities rise and fall with the sun, and are often like waves, in that they come and go. We are connected to the earth. You *have* heard the term "Mother Earth," right? This is by design. If you take care of mother, she will take care of you.

From day one, Mom was the emotional gatekeeper. Mother taught us our emotional standard and how to share by means of communicating. Even if that means sometimes communicating difficult feelings or emotions, we were encouraged to communicate.

HOW MEN ARE EMOTIONALLY DIFFERENT

Men were taught to suck it up: "Be bold. Be a man. Be hard. Men don't cry." Fathers love to teach their boys to be tough. They love to teach them to be aggressive. They scoff at any hint of an emotional outcry from their sons. If a little boy comes home from school crying because a bully beat him up, his father will usually give him two options: go back to school and kick that bully's ass, or get his ass kicked by dad!

Fathers often encourage violence and aggression in their sons. In football, there is nothing more "manly" than a 250-pound linebacker running as hard as he can into a 175-pound quarterback pummeling him! Boxing, fight clubs, video games, detachment—all of things are encouraged by men, and impressed upon and modeled for their little boys. Men value power. The entire notion of 'search and destroy' was developed by men, and it is encouraged in the workplace, in the home, *and* in the bedroom. Promiscuity is encouraged early-on, by men telling little boys that it's okay for them to bed as many girls as possible. They are also taught to be the breadwinners and to take care of home. And in the workplace, underhanded tactics and aggression in order to achieve dominance is admired.

WHEN A MAN HAS BEEN CASTRATED

A man who did not have a loving relationship with his mother—forgive me for saying so—is more likely than not to have issues with women, quietly resent them, or allow misogynistic behavior to rear its ugly head when it comes to them. He may not ever be able to admit this to himself, because it speaks to a very deep psychological imprint on his life—one he's likely not equipped to recognize and identify without professional help. But women often ask a potential mate about his relationship he has with his mother, in order to help them determine how he will treat them as his woman.

Conversely, if his mother is too overbearing, too involved in his life, too opinionated and has too much of a say in his decisions and path in life, he may grow to resent women, and find himself labeled a "mama's boy." I'm sure you're quite familiar with this phrase and have heard it used many times. Hopefully, though, it wasn't directed toward you. I personally have seen and dealt with a man dominated by his mother and the dynamic is quite fascinating.

Overbearing women do not allow a man to be a man. The "mama's boy" desperately *wants* to be a man, but his type of mother suppresses who he is, and prevents him from ever becoming a *real* man who can stand on his own. He wants to be loved, but he also wants to be respected. In some cultures, it is taught that at some crucial point, a son must leave his mother's arms and seek his wife's arms. If he does not choose to leave on his own, it is ultimately his mother's responsibility to kick him out of the nest. Hopefully, he will fly on his own. Overly-involved mothers, however, do not allow this.

WHY MEN FALL IN LOVE WITH THE WRONG WOMAN

When a man falls in love with a woman whose ways are similar to his mother's *negative* tendencies—for example, her stifling personality—there is an internal struggle that rages inside him. This prevents him from really loving that particular woman the way she needs to be loved. Such men lose their voices. As a result, these men are often referred to as "wimps," or as being "pussy whipped." They also tend to run from any type of conflict—these men are extremely **non-confrontational**. Again, they have swallowed their voices. And most likely, this "silenced" behavior is exhibited in all their adult relationships.

With all this being said, opposites do attract and can work well together. Still, as you can see, we are innately and inherently different (whether by design or otherwise). Understanding our individual foundations is paramount in knowing how to deal with each other appropriately. The great thing is we can work together the same way that our "parts" fit together.

CHAPTER 4

TRANSACTION HISTORY

Only 10 percent of how we behave in a relationship is based upon what is really occurring in that relationship. The other 90 percent is based upon what has happened to us in our childhood, and in our former romantic relationships!

What is your history, or your *baggage*? You hear talk shows throwing around the word "issues" all the time. It's the same thing. Loosely translated, it can mean a person is straight crazy! Seriously though, you may have heard the term "baggage" and decided it had nothing at all to do with you. You're wrong. We *all* have baggage. We were raised by imperfect people and no matter how much love they showed us, there's a strong likelihood that someone in our family screwed us up in some way, perhaps damaged us for life. The fortunate among us come to understand and acknowledge our "baggage," and our "issues." We successfully learn to identify and cope with them whenever they show up uninvited. In essence, we are dealing here with anything or anyone in our past that has been done to our psyche.

It's difficult for anyone, but for women, this is particularly tough, given that one out of four of us have been molested as children. These issues can affect our ability to trust men. It also may preclude us from being able to express the kind of vulnerability that is crucial for any intimate relationship. Some women are afraid to or can't express vulnerability, intimacy or trust because someone they trusted violated them.

For Black women in particular, the tendency to have abandonment issues is especially keen, given the fact that many of us were raised by our mothers in single-parent homes. We did not receive the love and acceptance from a male figure, leaving us with a vast emotional void. Being disappointed or abandoned in this way is beyond painful.

> **Promiscuous women desperately seek to fill this void by sleeping around with miscellaneous men. Women often use sex to get love. Sex is not love. But these women have an emotional deficit.**

A woman's self-esteem is instilled in her by her **father,** contrary to what most people think. When we have the love, respect, and adoration of a man early on in our lives, someone who tells us that we are beautiful, that we are relevant, that we are spectacular, that we are magnificent, that we are unique, that we are intelligent, and that we are worthy, does something our mother's love (as much-needed as it is, too) can't provide. If we get positive assurance and confirmation from a father figure, we are less inclined to seek this from assorted men. In fact, women with high self-esteem know they can do better than the man who is trying to pull them or beat them down. They won't allow themselves to be ranked second behind a wife or girlfriend. They won't accept being made to feel inferior in any way. They know they have healthier options. Such a woman's self-worth isn't tied to a dollar amount, or to the latest designer-logo handbag. She knows she deserves better, because her first love, her father figure, told her so.

Women who have been in abusive or failed relationships, who've been rejected, abandoned, or judged, are most vulnerable to the negative messages of her subconscious, which tell her she is unworthy of receiving love. She becomes afraid of being genuinely and lovingly supported. She will sometimes unknowingly push away the support of a good man. It is difficult for this type of woman to determine her worth. These feelings transform current, valid needs into desperate expressions, which ultimately turn men off.

Women with negative experiences in their past require a great deal of self-examination. They need to be honest with themselves when they do this, and perhaps even get a professional opinion. But these women are not hopeless. In fact, they can be the best type of woman for a man, because they have struggled, and know what the bottom feels like. Sometimes you can't appreciate good things unless you have experienced the bad. Now, I'm not advocating a man going upside a woman's head to give her a "bottom" experience, but the point is we all need to learn to appreciate a guy who's willing to wash the dishes. We need to recognize the inherent differences between us if we're going to have successful relationships.

LOOKS TIED TO INSECURITY

Some of the most beautiful women have the lowest self-esteem. How can this be? After all, our society seems to value a woman most for her appearance. We go on and on about how beautiful a woman is or how nice her body is, instead of how smart she is, how kind she is, or how successful she is. In fact, women possessing the same characteristics as a successful businessman—characteristics such as aggressiveness, assertiveness, and confidence—are labeled a "bitch." Women are told as little girls how pretty we are, how pretty a dress looks on us, or how nice we are and that we should always be nice. We are rewarded for this behavior. We are praised for looking and acting "pretty."

It is no wonder, then, that as we become women we turn these informal teachings into a belief system. We wear 5-inch stiletto heels—despite the studies that have shown that all kinds of back pain and physical ailments develop from wearing these types of shoes—to look appealing to men. In magazines, on television and in movies, we see how beautiful other women are. We understand that the first way a man typically describes a woman is by referring to how "fine" she is. Sadly, most men are usually more satisfied to have an uneducated beautiful woman on his arm, than to be with an average-looking educated woman. That's right, to most men, a fine-ass dumb girl trumps an average-looking girl who graduates cum laude.

Examples:

A very successful football player once told me that he **deserved** to have a beautiful wife. He actually used the word *deserved.* Another friend, a successful music mogul, stated that: "You are nothing without a fine woman by your side." It did not matter to him if she was a stripper or a woman with a questionable sexual history—i.e., a "ho"—just as long as she was a fine ho. She had the potential to become his wife, merely because of the way she looked. You have often heard the term "trophy wife." This, of course, is a woman who in society's eyes looks good on the arm of a very successful man.

Given such shallow norms, it should come as no surprise that a woman's self-esteem is tied to her looks.

So, when everyone is telling her she's the most beautiful woman they've ever seen—and she may even be a top model—this only fuels her insecurity. It is her beauty, ironically, that makes her most insecure. She may find herself questioning whether a more beautiful woman might come along and steal the man she cares for. This woman will more than likely question every move her man makes, every person he talks to, and everyone he looks at. She may constantly accuse her man of always cheating on her, or of never giving her enough attention.

An insecure woman may be envious of the close relationship you have with other women including long-time friends and even your very own mother.

This woman is so 'high maintenance', that even if you care for her, she will drive you insane with her annoying questions and accusations. You'll be lucky if she sabotages the relationship before she sets your house on fire in a fit of anger.

Jealousy and insecurity are the main reasons why women "hate" on other women the way they do. Every woman wants to feel like her man thinks she is the baddest chick on the planet. She wants to know that there is no other woman who can compete with her on any level whatsoever. Whether it is the way she looks, the way she cooks, her 'head game', her conversation, or how she takes care of her man, she wants to believe she's the best. Women are naturally competitive, as are men, but in a different way. Both sexes are capable of being jealous, but there are different things that trigger this emotion.

"Haters" are found among men and women, but I suspect that it was a man who first coined the term, and it was probably in reference to women he couldn't get. However, a woman is 10 times more likely than any man to spread gossip about other woman. She'll do this to make the other woman look bad so that you will never want to talk to her. She will be quick to say a beautiful woman is sporting a hair weave, breast implants, an imitation handbag—anything she can to cut another woman down. In fact, the only time women like this don't hate is when they don't perceive the other woman as a threat or when the woman is not intimidating. If the woman in question is *not* being "hated on," it may be that she's not in the insecure woman's age group, or she's a celebrity, or even that she's of another race. As such, she is not an immediate threat. Then (and only then) does the insecure woman sing the praises of another woman.

Men hate on other men by calling them a player, or a dog, or by saying they don't really have the wealth they project, or by saying they are no good. It is usually far less vicious than the tongue-lashing a woman can give, though. Unfortunately, insecurities are what bring out this behavior. Whether they're male or female, you must always consider what might be motivating a person to say nasty or hurtful things about another person. This behavior is never kind, nor is it ever justified, but it primarily has to do with the person's own personal struggle.

So, be careful not to come across as a hater or as an insecure man. That is the biggest turn-off for women. Always do you. Never worry about what another man may have and definitely don't let "player-haters" deter you from the woman you want.

WOMEN CONSTANTLY NEED VALIDATION

It's sad, but true. Even if you have already said something 20 times in a month, we may need to hear it another 20 times more. It should become a routine for a man. You should be able to anticipate when her insecurities start to surface and recognize it when you hear them or begin to see the signs. When this happens, the easiest fix is to do what you have to do or say to make her happy. It is really a small thing to sacrifice. When mama is happy, everybody is happy.

The good, the bad, and the ugly—well I'm not so sure about the ugly—in the end, you still love us and need us. Women are gentle and magnificent creatures, and should be treated with the utmost care. We are not to be physically or emotionally abused, stepped on, talked down to, or degraded in any manner. Rather, we are to be uplifted and put on pedestals where we belong. A woman who loves you will do anything for you—emotionally, physically, financially, sexually, and more, all without limitation. If you treat her with care, she will always be there for you and have your back through thick and thin. She will be that 'ride-or-die-chick', the Bonnie to your Clyde. The bottom line is, whether or not the relationship is successful or fails, if you have always been kind and forthright and respectful, you will have a friend for life at the end of the day.

CHAPTER 5

THE 80's LAKERS DYNASTY:
BRING SEXY BACK

The women have spoken and the results are in. So what do women find sexiest in a man? Contrary to what men believe, it's not the amount of money he has in his wallet, how wide his shoulders are, what he does for a living, or that he can throw his penis over his shoulder (as described by Eddie Murphy in his standup routine).

> ### The sexiest personality trait women find in a man is his confidence

That's *confidence*—not to be confused with conceit or arrogance. It is just the right combination of self-esteem and personal style. We call it his *swagger*. It's the way a man walks into a room—a way that commands attention, without him having to say a word. He is not desperate for your attention, he does not have to stand on his wallet to get respect, and he does not have to be flamboyant or boisterous to get people to notice him. He is not pressed to meet or push up on as many women as he possibly can. He is dynamic, and he exudes charisma. He is the man that women want to know. This is the very man that can get any woman he wants.

How can you get your girl? How long will it take?

There are two basic types of personalities men have that dictate how they will or if they approach a woman that catch their eye; A) the man that will not hesitate in his attempt to pursue that impossibly obtainable woman, or B) the man that will simply give up before he starts because he does not want to fail. Usually the man that will pursue the woman is a more powerful and/or successful man. He is a man of means. He is seasoned and has had his share of acquisitions in business and in his personal life. This man often times sees a woman as an acquisition. Can he have her? His bravado, his confidence, his self-esteem, and his swagger say, "Yes."

I've often joked about men who make a million and one excuses as to why they did not attempt to approach a women including not having enough money. The truth is this type of thinking is a natural filter in my selection process. I do not particularly look for men with a huge financial portfolio. But if you are the kind of man that would value who you are in relation to the highest dollar amount you can write on a check without it bouncing from here to China, then I, nor women like me, would not be interested in you anyway. By thinking this way, you have saved us all a lot of time.

WHY MEN FIND IT HARD TO APPROACH A WOMAN FOR THE FIRST TIME

Men fear rejection. Most men will say that the first time they approach a woman to engage her in conversation is hardest, simply because they do not know what type of reception they will get. When a man ventures into an unpredictable environment, such as a nightclub or other social scene, he can be immediately cast into a spotlight. His every move is measured and documented by the hundreds of eyes roaming the club. If he falls on his face, he has fallen on his face in front of countless people. If he gets shot down, sometimes it's something the entire room just saw. It's important to remember, though, that while the potential for disappointment here is high, the potential for success is equally great.

Other men are *more* extroverted, and don't mind rolling up on five women in one night, even if they don't have a shot with any of them. This type of man couldn't care less who is watching him, or how he is being perceived. But you do <u>not</u> have to be an extrovert to have confidence. There are some men who are naturally more shy and reserved, yet, are confident. Others are stifled by fear and anxiety. Either way, if you throw what might be a man's shyness into the mix, the degree of difficulty he faces in first approaching a woman is multiplied.

PEOPLE PROJECT INSECURITY

People scream to others that they are insecure by what they say and how they behave—through their physical actions. An insecure woman unsure of her attire, may constantly fidget, or tug on her dress all night. She may also repeatedly ask her friends if she looks okay, or frequent the ladies room to check herself out. One should always strive to feel comfortable about yourself, because if you don't, others will surely see it.

> **When approaching a woman, the number one rule of thumb is you must ALWAYS project confidence.**

Whether or not the woman of your choosing is receptive, you must know before saying a single word to her, that if she does not respond to you in a favorable manner, it is HER loss. She has no idea what she's missing.

CHEMISTRY IS SEXY

What is chemistry? Funny you should ask. Actually, it can be rather difficult to explain. But I'll take a crack at it. (*Not* a crack *addict*. LOL. Say them both together, and they sound they same. I *crack* myself up! ...No pun intended.) Where was I?... Right—at *chemistry*! Chemistry is: Part instant attraction, part feeling of similarity, part sensing of kindred spirits, or a feeling of familiarity and comfort. Chemistry is the sense of having an instant connection with someone, though you may not be able to put your finger on exactly why you like the person. You just know that you do. Some people try to relate this feeling to astrology and the "signs".

Personally, I'm not into agreeing with the Devil, but if *you* are, keep him at your house! LOL! Ok, seriously though: sometimes it's what a person reminds you of or makes you feel on a subconscious level that causes this feeling of "connection." The person is easy to talk to and you instantly feel like there is a bond or connection on a deeper level. Maybe he or she smells like a flower you love. Maybe their eyes remind you of your grandmother's. There are millions of possibilities, none with definitive answers. It's like God. Though you are unable to see Him, you know He exists.

GAME RULE #1
A real man doesn't have to lie

HONESTY IS THE ULTIMATE APHRODISIAC

I have spent countless hours debating this topic with men. A real man does not have to lie to get sex or a woman's attention. Women find honesty attractive. Most men, however, are convinced women do not really want to hear the truth—especially if "the truth" means divulging information she won't like, or might not handle well. Some men believe that by deceiving a woman, they are somehow protecting her from being hurt (along with protecting his own interests). Please—Give her the chance to make up <u>her own mind</u> about who you *really* are and what she wants to deal with. Even if you are married or in a relationship, you must tell her (Although my personal belief is that all women should run the other way when it comes to such immoral situations, as they usually end with someone being hurt or a family being torn apart). But if you *are* in this type of situation, it's your call, but still, you should at least give the woman the chance to determine whether and how she'd like to proceed. This is respectful, honest, and the right thing to do.

Here's an example: You meet a woman and she asks you, *"What do you want from me?"* (A question I will occasionally ask). Often, he may like to respond, *"I want to have sex with you."* But he knows that if he says exactly what he's thinking, he risks having to pick his teeth up off the floor! The key is, then, to be <u>*truthful,*</u> yet <u>*tactful.*</u> He may indeed want to sleep with the woman, so an honest yet appropriate answer would be, *"I am attracted to you, and I want to get to know you better."* Now it might very well be that he wants to get to know that **ass** a little better. But he is still being honest because he has said the same thing in a diplomatic way, and used honesty and decorum. Women are not fools; we know what this really means in "man speak." However, she can appreciate that this man had enough finesse and **game** to satisfy her with this answer, without deception or grossing her out.

Women will test you. And the easiest way to pass their tests is by being honest. Guys, I understand that this goes against the very grain of everything you've ever been taught by other men, but that is why you are reading **this** book. I am offering you a woman's point of view. You already know what *men* think, so here is a fresh take—what *women* are thinking. Women also have to "man up." We appreciate and respect an honest man!

IMPORTANT CHECK LIST: *BEFORE* YOU STEP TO A WOMAN

You would be surprised how many men take basic grooming for granted. Some of you more mature, evolved men may be insulted and look at these simple grooming habits as "grooming for dummies", however, I assure you that many of my sisters are still complaining, which means that many of you are slacking in this department. Remember, guys—don't turn her off before you can turn her on!

- Check your breath.

Brush, floss and gargle. You don't have to have perfect teeth, just make sure they are taken care of. If you neglect your teeth it will show in your breath. Teeth cleanings should be done by a dental hygienist every 6 months. I can't tell you how often women complain about someone being in their ears, and singeing the hairs in their nostrils.

- Take a shower.

Simple right? You'd be surprised how many men go from playing basketball to just washing up. They believe a splash of water and a change of clothes are enough. Not. Wash your ass! A bucket bath is not going to cut it.

- Wear clean underwear.

Whether they are tightie-whities or boxer briefs, keep them clean. I have seen guys wear the same, unwashed underwear when in a pinch. I am not even going to mention how nasty this is. Don't. Just stop. Bacteria lives and breeds in clothing. You naturally perspire, and also leave traces of <u>urine</u> and <u>feces</u> (track marks) in your

44

underwear, which are not always visible to the naked eye. You know your mother taught you better. Wear clean drawers!

- Do not use heavy cologne.

Cologne is not a substitute for a bath. It should also be used sparingly. One spray of cologne on your BODY is sufficient. She should only be able to smell you as you come close—not a whole ten minutes before you arrive and after you've gone. Another common complaint from women is when you men spray cologne directly on your clothing. If you are hugged or rubbed against, that woman is forced to wear your cologne, too—and Funky Old Medina does not smell good on a girl, or you for that matter. LOL!

- Iron your clothes.

Wash and wear does not mean *just that*. If your clothes have been washed, create a polished look by knocking the wrinkles out of your pants or shirt with a good old-fashioned ironing. Creases seem to be out of style for the most part, but you could at least keep the wrinkles away and use a lint roller to get those unwanted particles off your clothing.

- Dress appropriately.

Don't show up to dinner in a Nike track suit   I'm sure the latest Jordans look fresh to death on you, but there is nothing more aggravating to a women than taking the time to look great for you (which likely meant *hours* of preparation), only to be told the two of you can't be seated for dinner or allowed into a club because your brand-spanking-new sneakers had to make their debut. Clean out your car. No one wants to get into a messy car. If she has taken the time to look good for you the least you could do is clean out your car so she will have a place to sit her fine assets without thinking the ketchup stains on your seat from your last meal will ruin her lovely dress.

- Know where you are going.

It doesn't hurt to get directions ahead of time. At least you won't get lost and look foolish. Women want a man who is competent and getting her lost contradicts that.

- Have clean sheets on the bed.

You can never be too prepared. I have heard of men changing the sheets as soon as they bring a woman home. This looks suspect because we think to ourselves: *Did he just have sex on those sheets and need to change them?* Naturally that would be an immediate turn-off because now you have possibly ruined the mood. So save yourself some potential coitus interruptus.

- Clean your bedroom, kitchen and bathroom before going out.

Again, you have to be prepared for anything. Most company will hang out in your bathroom, den, or bedroom. And if you're lucky, she'll be in your kitchen the next morning, scrambling your eggs. Just hope they are not hot grits after your lack-luster performance ☺.

CHAPTER 6

TRYOUTS

Now that you have the basics down, it's time to hone your *approach*. You have your hygiene in check, the clothes and shoes are proper, and your confidence level is off the meter. It's time now to take some action. So you want to meet some girls, or go after the girl you have been ogling for some time, right? Here's where to go:

A FEW PLACES TO MEET WOMEN:

- Church
- Exercise class/Gyms
- Coffee shops
- Bookstores
- Library
- Beaches/Parks
- Concerts
- Museums
- Plays

- Restaurants
- Gyms
- Award shows
- Vacation
- Dog parks
- NBA All-Star
- Super Bowl
- Special gatherings
- Movie theaters
- Shopping malls
- Hair salons
- Nail salons
- Carwash
- Grocery stores
- Vegas
- Learning Annex
- Extended educational classes
- Cooking class
- Hosted dinners
- Workshops
- Apple Store/Classes
- Seminars
- Trade shows
- Group sports lessons
- Internet dating sites
- MySpace

WHAT TO SAY, WHEN TO SAY IT AND HOW TO SAY "IT"

> Unfortunately, women receive an abundant amount of unwanted attention on a daily basis. So we become tired of the pickup lines and are extremely defensive of any man that may approach us.

➢ *Ay bay bay, ay bay bay!*

➢ *Psssst. Pssssst. Pssssst.*

➢ *Hey, my friend wants to talk to you.*

➢ *Yo, mami! Come here for a second so I can holler at you!*

In case you are confused, all of the above are *poor* examples on how to approach women.

Other Turnoffs & Rules of How <u>NOT</u> To Approach A Woman:

- We are not animals do not cattle call at us.
- Hay is for horses.
- We cannot be beckoned with strange noises.
- We are not turned on by obscene gestures.
- Grabbing at your crotch while talking to us will make us think you have a sexually transmitted disease like crabs.
- We do not appreciate feeling like a piece of meat walking pass a construction site.
- No, we do not want to meet your friend!

- Do not pull along side us from your car asking us to come over. We are not Hookers.
- Do not grab our hand when we walk by or any part of our bodies. Five fingers will get you five in jail for assault.
- Do not get familiar with us by calling us baby or giving us a nickname as soon as you meet us.
- Corny pick-up lines never work if you are serious.
- Do not say or make overtly sexual comments about our bodies, what you want to do to us, or how you would do it.

WHAT WOMEN WANT

Women love to be chased—not stalked. I do not advocate behavior that might get you slapped with a restraining order. We like the phones calls, the e-mails, the IMs and the little things that let us know we are the objects of your desire. In this sense, we do not mind being objects, it is flattering. Women crave positive attention. We want to feel we are who you are vehemently pursuing. If you show her you are in to her, she will respond. Do this as long as she is being receptive to your advances.

SIGNS SHE IS BEING RECEPTIVE TO YOUR ADVANCES:

- She promptly returns your messages or e-mails.
- She seems happy or upbeat when you call.
- She makes time to speak to you.
- She is genuinely interested in what you have to say.

- She asks you questions about your personal life.
- She initiates contact.
- She shares personal things about herself when you do speak to her.
- She goes out on dates with you, if you have gotten that far.

Rule of thumb: pay attention to the signs.

Clues to look for that a woman is <u>not</u> available or is totally not feeling you:

- When you make direct eye contact with her she immediately rolls her eyes and looks away.
- As soon as you approach her she turns her back to you.
- She is standing with her girlfriend and she looks at you then whispers something in her ear and then they both start to laugh.
- She looks inebriated.
- She looks annoyed.
- She appears to be in a hurry.
- She is wearing a ring on her ring finger.

WOMEN PREFER THESE APPROACHES:

THE COMEDIAN

Humor <u>always</u> works! Women love to laugh and they love a man who can make them laugh. Corny lines and corny jokes only work if they are meant and said in a non-serious, tongue-in-cheek manner to intentionally make her chuckle. You might try saying three of them in a row to make it clear you are being silly...

- I know you are tired because you have been running around in my mind all day.
- I know your back is hurting because you just fell from heaven.
- If I could arrange the alphabet, "U" and "I" would be together.
- I hope you know CPR, because you are taking my breath away.
- Do you have a map because I keep getting lost in your eyes?
- I lost my number, can I have yours?
- Are you a parking ticket? Because you've got fine written all over you.
- Can I see your cell for a minute? I need to call my mom and tell her I just met the woman of my dreams.
- Let's go half on a baby.
- Do fries come with that shake?
- Are you from Tennessee? Because you are the only 10- I-see.

Be careful not to use "dirty" corny lines like, *Do you have any black in you? Would you like some?* That ain't funny! That's plain vulgar and rude! Coming across too familiar is a big turnoff as well. Keep it friendly, but don't act like her best friend. If she says her name is Samantha, for example, your next line should not be: "So, **Sam,** where are you from?" Women hate that! She didn't give you permission to call her a nickname. She just met you!

Keep it simple, stupid!

Hopefully, by using the recommended comedic approach, you'll immediately have her laughing or smiling, which will break the ice and help to let her defenses down. She'll be thinking, "He can't be all that bad."

Then perhaps you might offer to buy her a drink or casually continue to chat her up. Spend enough time talking with her, but not *too much* time, about 10 minutes max, just enough time to get her intrigued by you. By the time your 5 to 10 minutes of conversation are up, she should be on your hook—and on her cell phone telling her friends about the great guy she just met.

After you have made your introduction and piqued her curiosity, gracefully tell her it was a pleasure meeting her, ask if you can exchange email addresses or numbers, then exit. Make sure you disappear for the rest of the night. Don't hover around her for the rest of the night stalking her or gazing at her from afar. Simply say your peace and then leave.

> Remember, you have to at all times be in control, and always be willing to walk away. This is the real power move.

THE HIT AND RUN

This is by far the most widely-preferred method of introduction among the women we polled. Why do we call it the "hit and run?" Because of the smooth, unforeseen way a man will approach us, chats us up, and get our number and leaves…and we never even saw him coming!

Basically, the hit and run technique is when a man uses small talk as a way of initiating conversation with a woman. This method will not be easy for those of you who are not comfortable making general observations and comments. I am not speaking here of asking or making comments on the weather, but rather, of using your immediate environment as inspiration.

Example #1
Location: Club Setting
While standing at the bar you casually point out someone on the dance floor who is dancing crazy and say; "I see the new season of Dancing With The Stars has begun."

Example #2
Location: Car Wash.
"Which fragrance did you pick, pineapple or lavender? You look like the baby powder type."

Example #3
Location: Magazine stand.
"I hate it when people don't put the magazines back where they belong. You pick up a *Sporting Men Today* and a *Playgirl* with a dude spread eagle is staring back at you giving you the eye."

Example #4
Location: Coffee Shop
You need an interpreter just to order your coffee. Look at #5; the soy, non-fat, macchiato, sugar-free, mocha blended coffee with non-dairy whipped cream smoothie?

Get it? The idea is that it's completely casual. You are just making small talk, barely noticing her at all in the process. But that is the beauty in this approach. While you are busy making interesting small talk, she is engaged and relaxed while enjoying your witty conversation. She doesn't have to be on guard and you are giving her time to get a sense of who you are and learn that you seem like a decent guy. Never ask direct or personal questions. It can be a bit jolting coming from a stranger. Avoid walking up and introducing yourself because it's too abrupt not to mention stale. The key is subtlety.

Here, you want to give her your card, say you'd love to meet for coffee another time. Keep it simple and non-imposing. Or, you can also ask for her e-mail address. The less pressure you put on her, the easier it will be for her to say yes.

THE DISAPPEARING ACT

Ignore her. Well, not totally; just long enough to challenge her ego. If you have ever come to the conclusion that most women can be somewhat egotistical and self-centered, you are basically right in your assessment. Men like to chase, and women like being chased. When a woman encounters a man who appears to be unaffected by her $400 shoes, who doesn't notice the way her calves have the perfect curve ratio to her hips, she's offended yet challenged at the same time. You've no-doubt heard of (and may have even used) the pick-up strategy where a man will select the least-attractive girl at a party and show her a great time, "ignoring" the woman he *really* wants? Well, this actually works—in a reverse-psychology sort of way. By having a great time with the girl you don't actually prefer, you are showing the girl you *do* prefer that you are not so pressed to get to know her, and that you won't sweat her like everyone else in the club. You're also challenging her ego this way. She's now thinking (if you are actually on her radar, that is), *"Am I able to get this man's attention? What is he about? Why isn't he noticing me?"* She will then make it her business to "conquer" you. And there is your opportunity to close the deal.

After a night of having a great time with another woman, casually approach her. Make as little eye contact with her as possible. She will find a way to strike up a conversation with you. Or you might casually notice her great shoes, complimenting her on them. See if she bites. Usually, she will—and she will be putty in your hands, as long as you maintain your confidence.

THE INTRODUCTION

Using your friends is probably the easiest and safest way to introduce yourself to the girl you desire. Try to make it a casual or a happenstance meeting. Have your friend arrange for the two of you to be in the same place at the same time, but where it isn't obvious you have been waiting on her to show. When she arrives, it'll be more like, *Oh, Nancy, have you met my friend, Joe?* Voila! Not much work at all. You are just hanging out, and not pressed to meet anyone. Just kick it with her for a minute, making sure to leave for a while, then, come back to her just before you leave to say your good-byes and offer her your number or card. Never go straight in for the kill. By casually visiting with her, it affords her the opportunity to warm up to you and develop a sense of rapport and chemistry, all without any pressure. Be fun and exciting, and you'll be able to charm the pants off of her. *Literally.*

ASKING FOR HER NUMBER VS. GIVING HER YOURS

I prefer if a man asks me for what is the best way for us to keep in touch. This way, I have a choice. I can give him my number if I choose, then, gauge how interested he is in getting to know me by his attempts to further get acquainted. Again, women like to be chased, and I'm all for getting caught!

The other side of this coin is to make a woman feel comfortable. Giving her your card may be more acceptable to her than directly asking for her number. But then again, if she happens to lose it (as I have done on occasion), you will have no way of really knowing what happened. My recommendation then is that you ask for her number and/or e-mail, and also give her your card.

Now that you have the digits, you want to know how long to wait to call her? I promise you, I have given a man my number, and within *twenty minutes,* he's called me! I then proceed to deposit his number in the nearest trash can. Why? Because of his clear desperation—*so* not sexy *and* a complete turnoff! Couldn't a brother at least wait till he got home? Never mind waiting to get home, wait at least a few days before you call her. Three days is the perfect wait-time; you have to assume that a man who has something to offer a woman has options. He may be working, he may be busy, or he may be dating other women. It makes sense that he would take a few days to call or e-mail to get better acquainted. I immediately recognize that he has *game*, and that he has options. And that, subconsciously, puts him in the forefront of my mind.

FLAG ON PLAY: When you do call, don't be in the middle of a football game commercial or riding in a car with a bunch of raucous friends. Just take five minutes to focus on her. If your friends act a fool, she will think you are silly. If you can't take 5 minutes to focus on her alone, you are already communicating to her that she is not worth your time. Also, don't wait more than a week to call. I had someone call after six months. He actually thought I would remember him! Even if I did, the nerve of him to think I would still give him a chance. Not sexy, 6 months? He was long forgotten. As B.B. King said, *"the thrill was gone!"*

Here's a general outline on how to play it safe. Focus on being interesting and not making her think you are a total Looney Tune or Bug-a-Boo. Keep it simple. Keep the dates and conversations short. Keep the focus on her.

GAME RULES OF COMMUNICATION IN THE **FIRST MONTH:**

- Don't call a woman more than three times without getting a return call.
- Don't call a woman more than twice a week after meeting her.

- Don't send multiple UNANSWERED e-mails or text messages.
- Don't spend more than 15 minutes talking to her in initial conversations.
- Don't spend more than 3 conversations with her before asking her out.
- Don't tell her your life story when getting acquainted.
- Don't reveal in the first 3 months that you have always wanted to date her if you have.
- Don't talk about marriage or past relationships in the first month unless she directly asks you.
- Don't reveal your problems or disappointments or family dysfunction.
- Don't share your baby mama drama with her.
- Don't reveal your salary.
- Don't brag about your alleged sexual prowess.
- Don't name drop. Keep your celebrity friends to yourself.
- Don't introduce her to your entire family.
- Don't introduce her to your children.
- Don't reveal how many times you have been dumped.
- Don't be too available when she calls.
- Don't complain about your life.
- Always be positive.
- Don't take her as your date to a wedding.
- Never complain or point out things you don't like about her.

Remember, this advice is to be used for the good of both sexes. Not for your own get-kitty-quick-schemes.

CHAPTER 7

THE PLAYERS

There are many varieties of ladies so know your prize.

THE VETERAN

AKA, *The Older Woman.* Who can't appreciate a wealth of knowledge and vast experience? Don't be intimidated by an older woman. The more experience she has, the more she can teach you—if you are open to being taught. Not saying that she has to stand up in front of a blackboard with chalk in hand, pointing out the lessons of the day. All you have to do is watch, listen and learn young buck. It may be as simple as how she carries herself or the little nuances in her conversation and attitude; one way or another, she's likely to teach you things you didn't realize you wanted to learn. An aggressive, ambitious, successful, attractive woman who knows what she wants and knows how to get it never goes out of style.

The Older Woman…

<u>Pros:</u>

- More mature
- Better lovers
- Can teach you a thing or two
- Financially stable
- More direct
- Easier to deal with/less drama
- In her sexual prime
- Likes younger men for sexual partners
- Knows what she likes/wants
- Knows how to express herself and communicates easily
- Knows herself better and how to relate to various kinds of men

<u>Cons:</u>

- May want marriage and not casual dating
- May only desire a casual relationship and not marriage
- May want children if she has none
- Tired of games/cuts to the chase so there is no room for error
- More baggage
- May have older children who do not like the idea of their mother dating someone close to their age

THE POINT GUARD

AKA, *The Wealthy and Successful Woman*. Although all women are different, we all have one need—the need to be loved. Let's use one of my favorite role models as the archetype: Oprah Winfrey. Ms. Winfrey is a strong, powerful, intelligent, well-traveled, well-versed, highly intellectual, spiritual, wealthy and articulate WOMAN. She can buy anything her heart desires. But that only encompasses a material need. What is her emotional need? She may have great family or even wonderful friends that provide emotional support and a strong foundation for her. Many people may think women of her stature don't need anything from a man per se. This couldn't be farther from the truth.

Money cannot replace a man. Success cannot replace a man. Again, this speaks to the natural order of things. A woman who knows what she wants professionally and materialistically, and has acquired those things and reached those goals in life, still needs and may desire fulfilling companionship and/or a relationship with the opposite sex. Money cannot give you children. Money cannot give you companionship. Money cannot provide stimulating conversation and healthy debates. Money cannot be your shoulder to cry all on when the world is too much to bear. Money cannot make love to you or give you multiple screaming orgasms. Money cannot make you feel safe and protected. And most important, money can't love you.

The Wealthy and Successful Woman...

<u>Pros:</u>
- Independent
- Doesn't need your money
- Can pay for her own way (and yours)
- May desire companionship

<u>Cons:</u>

- May be used to being in control
- May be impatient
- May be spoiled
- May be defensive to the true intentions of strangers or new male friends

THE GROUPIE

AKA, *The Jump Off.* If she lets you call her at 3 a.m. from the club to "come by and get a hug", without ever taking her out in public, then you can surmise that this may be a woman who does not respect herself, so she accepts being the J.O.

However, if she curses you out and tells you to call at a decent time or don't call at all, then this is more than likely a woman with some standards. Or, since this is the year 2007 and the world seems morally bankrupt, she may not want a deeper commitment. This woman doesn't mind being the casual "thing." She is the down for whatever whenever girl. She may just work at the W Hotel.

The Jump Off...

Pros:

- Most likely down for whatever
- You can call her whenever you want
- Is usually a cheap date
- She knows her place
- May be good in bed
- May be a bigger freak in bed

Cons:

- Can't take her in public
- May become attached
- May be a bigger sexual health risk

THE FRANCHISE PLAYER

AKA, *The Celebrity or Famous Woman*. If you decide to speak to a celebrity, bring your **A** game and keep in mind that timing is everything.

Jennifer Lopez, Halle Berry, Salma Hayek, Naomi Campbell, Beyoncé, the latest Video Vixen, or the popular Actress of the day—are all women whom you may have enjoyed gluing countless pages of magazines together in the privacy of your bathroom at the very thought of ever touching them in real life.

This woman is the ultimate prize. She is the trophy girl, the impossible one, every man's fantasy. But what if, just what if, you ever had the opportunity to meet her? Perhaps you are the runner at the law firm she has on retainer. Maybe you are her friend's brother's cousin' uncle's friend? Maybe you are an up-and-coming artist who occasionally runs in the same circle as she? Do you have a chance with her? Well, the answer is simple. **Maybe**. Never say never.

It is your world but timing is everything. She may be between marriages, dumped by her last star football player boyfriend, or she may just go for the regular Joe to keep her "tuned up" on the regular and discreetly out of the probing lenses of the paparazzi.

There is *always* a chance. So if ever given the opportunity, go for it using the same application from chapter one. Be confident. Let her know that neither her celebrity nor her money intimidate you.

Follow these guidelines:

- Do not pretend like you don't know who she is or what she does for a living, especially if she is on TV everyday or constantly in the news or magazines.
- Do compliment her. Tell her she is striking on film or TV, but in person, she is even more attractive and her spirit is very powerful.
- Do give her your phone number. Trust, if she is feeling you or even thinking about it, she will not necessarily want to give you her number. There are too many stalkers and nut jobs out there. You have to put the ball in her court.
- Do ask her for a MAILING ADDRESS. Tell her you'd like to send her something.
- Follow up with flowers or a special well thought-out gift. Make sure your number is included and remind her how she met you on a sweet note.
- If you do have any contact with her, store her personal info under a different name. For example, if her name is Tyra Banks, store it under Tyrone Banks. Don't take any chances

with her privacy. Having your goofy friends post her number on the internet is not a good look.

- Keep the conversations fairly short. No longer than 15 minutes at a time.
- Get her to agree to a date after you sense she is somewhat comfortable with you.
- Invite her to a non-public place or, over for dinner? If you can cook, man that is sexy!
- Invite her over to watch a movie and serve good wine.
- Drive her to a private park, or romantic lookout or scenic area.
- Ask her out for coffee. Any place that is fairly private and she won't be harassed by fans is good.
- If you are a man of means, you can get really creative here. You can rent out an entire small restaurant, movie theater, skating rink—the possibilities are only limited to your imagination. For example, if you invite her over, hire a private chef. This will make her feel more at ease and special.
- Don't try to make the first move.
- Do not withhold compliments. The biggest mistake men make is to withhold compliments from model-types or celebrity women. You take the position that everyone else says it to her and you want to be different. Wrong! Women receive compliments differently from whoever pays them to her. Treat her the same way as you would anyone else.

TO GOOGLE OR NOT TO GOOGLE

That is the question. Be careful of knowing too much about her that she hasn't shared with you. With the information superhighway always rearing its ugly head, it's so tempting to try and find out every single thing about a person you admire.

The problem with this is you will inevitably reveal details about her in conversation she has never divulged to you. She will know it and you will look like a fan. If she sees you as a fan, she will never be comfortable enough to date or hang out with you. Discovery is the best part of the relationship. Take pleasure in finding those things out from her if given the opportunity.

The Celebrity/Famous Woman...

Pros:

- Well traveled
- You can share her perks of the trade
- Independent
- Usually creative
- Exciting to be with
- Usually less inhibited

Cons:

- Has privacy issues that may often interfere with spontaneity
- Most are spoiled
- Has many options when it comes to men
- Usually distrustful of a man's motives
- May treat you with less respect than her celebrity boyfriends
- Most are eccentric AKA crazy as hell

THE RETIREE

AKA, *The Married Woman*. I am not one to advocate setting your sights on a married woman. I believe in honesty. If a woman is unhappy, she should seek counseling with her husband or seek a legal separation or divorce. The love triangle is not to be taken lightly. Dating a married woman is not advisable. Not only is it immoral and despicable, it's dangerous. I'm not talking about the type of danger when you are making love in an elevator dangerous. I mean you have a shotgun pointed between your eyes by her husband dangerous. You are corrupting a special bond made before God. There could be children involved and emotions run high.

By dealing with a married woman, you are only inviting drama and potential bodily harm to yourself for banging another man's wife. Watch out for the karma headed your way. There is a plethora of unmarried, single women in the world. Find one of those.

The Married Woman...

Pros:
- None

Cons:
- Possible death or severe dismemberment

Whichever woman you chose, you must first win over her heart.

HOW TO WIN OVER A WOMAN'S HEART

- Be sincere
- Win over her friends

- Win over her mother and father
- Be unique
- Be interesting
- Be patient

WOMEN LIKE GIFTS

It's Valentine's Day and she is angry because you bought her the vacuum cleaner she said she wanted the last time you were at Target. You can't understand why she is so angry because she did say at some point and time that she wanted it. So why is she tripping? You have to know the difference between a romantic gift and a "just because" gift. A woman wants romance. She wants to be thought of as loved and desired. A vacuum cleaner as a gift on Valentine's Day says, you remind me of my housekeeper. That is not sexy.

Romantic gifts can be small or large, just make sure that they are loving in nature.

Women consider these gifts as romantic:

- Poetry
- Flowers
- Handwritten notes or letters
- Jewelry
- Trips/vacations
- Spa certificates
- Stuffed animals
- Lingerie
- Photographs
- Chocolates/candy

- Perfume
- Wine/champagne
- Dance lessons for couples
- Romantic board/card games
- Naughty sex toys
- Romantic movies
- Romantic CDs
- Shoes
- Clothes
- Furs
- Big ticket items i.e. cars, houses, condos, etc.

The "just because" gifts can be anything. But here is a clue on how to win her over with your selections: LISTEN.

My favorite gifts have always been from men who listen for the clues. It's hard to guess what a woman likes. Women do not have to try to listen. We record in our minds when a friend, male or female, says they like something. Whether it is a pair of shoes she sees while casually strumming though a magazine, or a pair of earrings she says she lost, these are the clues for what to buy her as a gift when the time comes. With listening, you can never go wrong because she has already told you what she wants without knowing it. Just file it away in your mind and when gift-giving time comes you are already ahead of the game.

One of my very favorite gifts came from a friend who was a master at gift giving. He was an only child raised by his mother so I believe he had an advantage when it came to understanding women. In conversations he asked me what my favorite movie was and I told him. He knew that I collected vintage movie posters and did not have one from my favorite movie. On Valentine's Day a package arrived from France. When I opened it I was ecstatic. He had not only found the movie poster of my dreams that was out of print and unavailable in the States, he had taken the time to have it framed for me. It was so special and I was very appreciative of his efforts.

Another gift was from a best friend at Christmas. She knew from a previous conversation that I needed some pajamas. She already knew the colors I liked and she surprised me with a sumptuous pair of fleece pajamas from Target, or Targét as I like to call it, in my favorite color. I know, not sexy, but for the alone nights they are perfect. So again, it is not the price of the gift it is the thought behind it.

Never be afraid to ask her what she wants. I'm a woman who doesn't mind being asked. I love a gift certificate to my favorite store or spa because then I can get what I want and the money is well spent. What woman does not want to go to a spa? She will be relaxed and pampered and when she is there she will be thinking of the person who is responsible for her luxurious day.

I'd prefer to have someone tell me what they want. There is nothing worse than a gift you do not like or can't use. People say it is the thought that counts. But a yearly subscription to the fruit cake monthly delivery club is a waste of money for someone who hates fruitcake. I don't like to waste money nor do I want someone else to. You have to remember, the gift is not about the monetary value, it is the foresight and insight that counts.

The worse gifts are when a person gives you what *they* want versus what *you* want. Although they mean well, it is selfish in a way. You have to think of what the recipient would like and not what you would like. For instance, I had an ex with a knack for this. I once said I played the violin when I was growing up but did not have the patience or **desire** to pick one up again. At the next holiday he bought me an electronic violin and said I needed to revisit my lessons. True story!

The same ex. If I said I did not like something, he would buy it for me. Although I greatly appreciated him being the kind of man who wanted to make me happy by giving me small tokens of his love, he made me feel bad because he would deliberately go against what he already knew, without a shadow of a doubt, I would NOT like. It became such an issue that I never wanted him to give me anything because I could never hide my disappointment and I never wanted to hurt him.

I absolutely was grateful for him. But because he would purposely or subconsciously sabotage his efforts, neither one of us appreciated the other. It didn't matter the cost of the items. If I always walked away thinking this man had a deeper issue with me, and the gift was a part of a more profound character flaw or disconnect in our relationship, then he would never be appreciated and money had absolutely nothing to do with it.

In short, learn your woman. Listen to her hints. The price of the gift is inconsequential, it is the forethought behind it that matters most.

CHAPTER 8

HOW TO SCORE

THE EASIEST WAY TO GET SEX IS NOT TO TRY

Listen and learn; the easiest way to get sex is not to try to get sex. I know this goes against what you think. **Women usually decide if they want to sleep with you within the first five minutes of meeting you.** It is either a yes, absolutely no, or maybe. If you fall into the "absolutely no" category you will understand that immediately. She will not give you the time of day. If you happen to fall into the "absolutely yes" category, then you are a lucky bastard! This usually means that she has an immediate and strong physical attraction to you, coupled with that is her sexual desire. Depending on what type of woman she is, it is just a matter of opportunity and timing for her to sleep with you. She will let you know through her words, body language and actions that she wants to make it happen. The easiest way and fastest way is to not come on to her too soon. Show her you are interested—yes. Show her you like her—yes. But do not try to get her out of her clothes.

Do **not** give her a kiss on the first date other than something small. If the opportunity presents itself for you to sleep in the same bed with her, and if you have any self-control, do so without touching her one time throughout the night. If it means that you have to visit the little boy's room with your favorite pin-up girl to help you accomplish your goal, do it. The dividends will pay off later. She may find your chivalry completely irresistible and try to jump your bones by the time you both wake up. Most women can appreciate a man with self control.

Now if you fall into the "maybe" category, you have to show her why you are a good look.

Women primarily plan to have sex. We have made up our minds long before you arrive to pick us up whether you are getting any that night.

We shave our legs, wear pretty underwear, wax, and grease our bodies up for the festivities to come. We will have that extra glass of wine and make sure our calendar is clear for the morning after. Men on the other hand, just need the wind to blow in their vicinity to be ready for sex. So the key factor to remember is the *seduction*. It is not with her body, it starts with her mind by winning her over.

SIGNS THAT A WOMAN IS READY TO HAVE SEX

- She seems really into you.
- She asks you about other sexual partners.
- She asks what you have to do the next morning.
- She has that extra glass of wine on your date.
- She hangs on your every word.
- She asks you about your last check-up.

- She asks you about your HIV status.
- She asks you to get tested with her.

HOW TO GET HER OPEN

➢ Get her to like you and like your company.
When you are out be yourself. Don't linger on your hang-ups. Present the person you really are. She should see the genuine article and like what she sees. Remain confident and show no signs of intimidation.
➢ Always compliment her.
Let her know if she is looking extra fine or notice her new hair style. Always tell her you had a good time after a date if you did. Tell her you can't wait to see her again.
➢ Women love affection.
Don't be afraid to touch her. Get her used to thinking about you in a sexual way. Whether that means holding her hand every now and then, or giving her a tight and sensual hug, make sure your focus is always on her. She will sense that you are attracted to her and this gives her confidence.
➢ Every now and then, be mannish.
I'm a sucker for a strong man. I'm a big girl, so I like to know a guy can manhandle me if he needs to, speaking in a playful way of course. If a man I'm with suddenly picks me up and lightly slams me against a wall, I'm extremely turned on. I love to be picked up, something that may be a little strange, but hey, different strokes right? Flex on her from time to time by showing off the reason you have those bulging biceps you worked so hard to get. Let her feel a flash of the heat between you. Women like strength, so don't be afraid to show it off. Wrestling or play fighting is great for this too. You get to position her in all kind of ways in the name of fun, and you can be a little naughty

with it. Trust, she will be thinking about how nasty-good you might be in bed.

➤ Every now and then grab her ass inappropriately.

Women like a respectful guy so don't go crazy with this one. This should not occur on the first few dates. But a light pat or gentle cupping during a hug is ultra sexy. Affection is always welcomed especially when you don't see it coming.

➤ Say something dirty to her but not obscene, just a little off the cuff.

This is part of the dance. We invited you, now dance. It's just testing the boundaries. We're cracking the door just a taste to look inside. Innuendo is fine, but don't dive in. Just get your feet wet. Later you can concentrate on getting her wet.

➤ Keep in contact with short messages/text messages or emails.

Let her know she is on your mind. Do not attempt to write a book on her cell phone. Just a "hey I miss the way you smell" will drive her insane.

➤ Don't be corny. No mixed tapes or CDs at first.

You can cleverly make a tape and play it while she is visiting or during the ride in the car. If she asks about it, burn one for her. It is a great "just because" gift. Don't make it a big presentation. Leave it on her kitchen counter or car seat with a little note. Also, take her to see her favorite concert. Lyrics to songs can be too much to handle if they are too romantic. I once had a guy after some time of knowing him confess his feelings for me through a CD. It was impressive because it wasn't mushy, and it was romantic and thoughtful because he happened to have excellent taste in music. I still play that CD because it is so hot. But if you are just getting to know her, try buying a CD of her favorite artist but no mixed tapes, they reveal too much.

➤ Never forget her birthday.

If you want to turn a woman completely off, then forget her birthday. To be safe, plan ahead. Never ever forget a woman's birthday or Valentine's Day. No matter where you are in the relationship, send her a gift. Whether it is a bottle of her favorite wine or a teddy bear, or a book, always send her something. You get points for having it wrapped. We like to see that you have taken the time to do something special for us. This makes us feel special in turn. It is a warming up process and she will appreciate the gesture.

➤ Pay attention to what she says she likes.

This small show of interest will gain points quickly. Be genuinely interested. We touched on this in previous chapters. Do listen. If you listen carefully enough, you may hear her thong drop on the floor.

➤ Go places she wants to go.

Ask her what she wants to do or places she would like to go. Go out of your way to plan something that she likes. Mad points for this!

➤ Do something she has never done with anyone else.

This is a part of discovery. If she has never been horseback riding, take her. If she has never been to wine country, plan a day trip. The small things will make you pull ahead of the heap.

➤ Call her frequently at first.

Call her in the beginning of the relationship then abruptly not call her for a week. This is all part of the tease. If she gets used to you and you become predictable, she may lose interest. By breaking the rhythm, you will bring out her true feelings about you. When you return, hopefully she will have missed you and feel appreciative of you being there. This is only in the beginning. After the relationship is established, this suggestion does not apply.

➤ Sensually embrace her.

Let her feel your body and smell good while doing it. Women who love men, love to be embraced by a man. Just as you like to feel our bodies against you, women love to feel your body too. Maybe if it is sensual enough, she will feel your package and become a little more curious.

HOW TO RACK UP POINTS WITH A WOMAN

1. Turn your damn cell phone off while on a date.
2. Only focus on her when you are with her.
3. Make eye contact when speaking to her. Don't pretend like you didn't see a fine woman walk into the room. See the fine woman, and tell her that woman doesn't have anything on her.
4. Make her feel like she is your dream girl.
5. Notice when she changes her hair and compliment her.
6. Notice and compliment a new pair of shoes.
7. Take her on a picnic.
8. Hold her hand while lying in bed together.
9. Cook a meal for her.
10. Serve her breakfast in bed.
11. Draw a bubble bath for her.
12. Wash her hair.
13. Find out what her favorite flowers are and send them for no reason.
14. Send her thoughtful emails.
15. Never ever forget her birthday and plan ahead.

16. Never forget Valentine's Day and send her a present well in advance.
17. Call her mother on her birthday or send her mother flowers thanking her for raising such a beautiful woman.
18. Give her a massage.
19. Rub her back when she is agitated.
20. Give her a hug for no reason.
21. After a night of being out or a hard day of work, take off her shoes and rub her feet.
22. Offer to run an errand for her.
23. Surprise her at the office to take her to lunch and bring a single flower.
24. Offer to fix something around her house.
25. Tell her what your favorite part of her body is.
26. Whisper in her ear how sexy she is.
27. Tell her a certain song reminds you of her.
28. Play the song for her as a message without your voice on her answering service.
29. Tell her if/when you are going to be late.
30. If you travel, call her to tell her you made it safely.
31. Have phone sex with her.
32. Always ask her how her day was.
33. Tell her you admire her and why.
34. If she does not like a part of her body, make sure you tell her it is just as beautiful as the rest of her.
35. Take her someplace she has never been.
36. Take her out on dates that you plan.
37. Never be predictable.
38. Get to know her friends.
39. Show her *small* public displays of affection (PDAs) especially in front of her friends, being careful not to go overboard or make anyone feel uncomfortable.

40. Wash the dishes and/or clean up after she has cooked you a meal.
41. Make sure to thank her for cooking for you.
42. Always make her feel appreciated by saying thank you for the small acts of kindness she shows toward you.
43. Tell her how much you appreciate her for no reason.
44. Show her that her friendship means more to you than anything else she could give you.
45. Sleep in the bed with her once without trying to have sex with her.
46. Give her oral sex without expecting or getting anything sexual in return.
47. Tell her a corny joke.
48. Tell her a sexy joke.
49. When meeting her in a bar, as a game, pretend like you are a stranger and try to pick her up.
50. Tell her about a fantasy that you have that she stars in.
51. Frame a picture of her and display it in your house or at work where she can see it when she visits.
52. Leave the toilet seat down in the bathroom.
53. Pick up your clothes around the house.
54. Stay neat and clean.
55. Take her on a long drive.
56. Take a shower before sex.
57. If you have to use her bathroom for other than urinating, try to use a bathroom farthest away from her and make sure to air spray or light a candle.
58. Let her choose cologne for you that she likes and wear it for her.
59. Always pull out her chair.
60. Place her napkin on her lap while dining.

61. Open doors for her.
62. Carry heavy items/bags for her.
63. Do not pass gas in front of her.
64. Have good table manners.
65. After sex, bring her a warm towel.
66. Always greet her with a kiss or affection.
67. Feed her chocolate or fruit like strawberries.
68. Pay a bill for her.
69. Wash the dishes without being asked.
70. Always pump the gas in her car for her.
71. Get her oil changed for her.
72. Make a charitable contribution in her name.
73. Help her repair her credit if needed.
74. Accompany her to make a large purchase.
75. Use a photo of her as a screen saver.
76. Pick up the bill if you are out with her friends.
77. Double date with her.
78. Approach her from behind and kiss her on her neck.
79. Walk her dog.
80. Write a hook in a song about her.
81. Do a crossword puzzle together.
82. Take her golfing with you.
83. Take her for a walk, bike ride or hiking.
84. Take her on a motorcycle ride.
85. Play touch football with her.
86. Buy a pair of panties for her and put them in her drawer with a note saying her ass would look great in them.
87. Buy her a journal or photo album to keep memories in.
88. Kiss her on her forehead.
89. Take a night swim or Jacuzzi naked.

90. Take the time to teach her a card game like Poker of Black Jack.
91. Make coffee for her in the morning.
92. Place post-its in random places with sweet thoughts written on them.
93. Always dress well and appropriately for the occasion.
94. Always be on time.
95. Never pressure her for sex.
96. Never get jealous.
97. Always support her ideas. If there is a way to help her accomplish her goals, do.
98. Bring in the paper with her robe and coffee in the morning.
99. Help her children with homework.
100. Send her mother and/or daughter flowers on Valentine's Day.

These are just a few things that women adore in a man. There are no limits to how creative or thoughtful you should be. The sky is the limit.

HOW TO LOSE POINTS WITH A WOMAN: TOP 10

1. Giving her a backhanded compliment.
I get this all the time. Strangers will approach me and say: "You look different in person." My response is often: "Ok, I don't know how to take that." I ask myself if they are saying I look good on TV and jacked up in person, or, if I look great in person and jacked up on TV? Either way, it just doesn't come across well. Remember, always state things in a positive way. In this instance, one can simply say, "You are more beautiful in person." This way you don't convolute the intent.

- **FLAG ON THE PLAY**: ON COMPLIMENTING DARK SKINNED WOMEN

Okay, this is definitely a pet peeve of mine, and will quickly get a man black-listed in my book. Being a dark-skinned woman, oftentimes, men will inadvertently devalue our beauty. For example, they will say things like, "You are pretty *to be dark*," or, "You are the finest *dark-skinned* woman I have ever seen." Although a guy may not mean these statements in a derogatory way, we most **always** take it that way. I even had a man say to me recently, "I'm usually not attracted to dark-skinned women."

When ignorant comments like these are made, what dark-skinned Black women hear is, "Your type (meaning dark-skinned women) is really not as fine as a light-skinned girl," and "I normally don't like women of your complexion, so you should feel honored and privileged that I like you." And also we hear, "You will never be my dream girl, because you look the way you do. Therefore, I will always find someone of lighter skin more attractive than you," Lastly we hear, "You are not good enough for me, really, because my preference is light skin— something you will never be."

It's too difficult a task to give people who make distinctions and statements like these a history lesson on slavery and color consciousness that exist in the Black community, in our country, and in the world, but I'll try.

Going back in history, Black people were made to feel ashamed by slave masters and slave makers for being dark, and for having kinky hair and for our wide noses. "Mulattos," or mixed-race Blacks were celebrated and rewarded for their beauty, while the "darkies" were made to work the fields and wore the mulatto's hand-me-down clothes. In fact, the dark-skinned slaves were not allowed inside the masters' homes. Similarly, many of us are painfully too acquainted with the proverbial "you-so-black" jokes used to taunt, torment, and shame darker-skinned children, even to this day.

Sadly, the seed of such self-hatred remains deeply ingrained in many of us, yet, acknowledging this fact is key to identifying—and denouncing—hurtful and demeaning comments on our dark-skinned sisters' (and brothers') complexions. The aforementioned pseudo compliments on deeper-hued women are no different.

Pretty is pretty, and attractive is attractive—regardless of one's placement on the color wheel. Even if you feel as the men from my real-life examples felt, there is no need to express this to someone you are romantically interested in, nor to what might be your dark-skinned child, for that matter. You need to be sensitive about these latent, racist points of view that most of us still can't acknowledge we still carry around with us. Obviously, a person cannot change his/her skin color. And most importantly, all shades of Black are beautiful, and should be celebrated and revered. **Never,** *ever* say such ignorant things to a woman! Whether she actually makes you aware of the humiliation she feels or not, while commenting on the exceptionality of her beauty, she will most certainly harbor resentment toward you for saying it, *or* say nothing at all, but leave quietly wounded by what you have said.

2. Being negative or putting a woman down.

After spending a weekend visiting someone whom I adored from numerous conversations in an attempt to get to know him better, upon leaving, he sent me several text messages that read like the following: "I like who you can be, not who you ARE or WERE (titles, etc.). He went on to say how, "I was not living up to my full potential" AND to add insult to injury, he said he thought, "I can be so much more than I am." I told him that his comments were insulting to me and he further concluded, "I figured you would take it that way." I thought to myself, "Well what way could anyone have taken such remarks?"

Although I was put off, hurt, and taken aback by his insensitive and judgmental statements, I didn't retaliate. I *could* have asked him to step off the water he was walking on. I *could* have pointed out his obvious flaws. He was short, overweight, minimally attractive, has enormous buck teeth, is a 42-year-old divorcee living with his Mother, and has a child from a former girlfriend—not from his marriage that lasted a mere 2 years. He simply wasn't the prize he thought he was. I choose not to say things out of anger because that is not who I am. I am not going to be that angry/hurt Black woman who tears a brother down. Everyone has flaws, I certainly am not perfect, and neither is anyone else. But I liked him before he said those things. I saw the flaws, true, but I was more interested in his potential. Obviously, no woman can respond positively to someone who viciously puts her down so he can feel better about himself. Big red flag!

The point here is simple; **never try to tear a woman down,** even if there are things about her you do not like or think she can improve on.

A man can get a woman to do almost anything if he does it with finesse, love and kindness. Whether he wants to motivate her to go back to school, get a job, or encourage her to live her dreams, he must do it in a supportive way where she feels uplifted, adored and respected by the man she loves. A good man can

GENTLY teach, guide, encourage, persuade, empower and grow WITH her until they EACH reach their full potential, individually, and as a couple. Condescending statements never support nor uplift anyone.

3. Having someone spend the night in your home while she is visiting.

If she is visiting you from out of town, don't have your female friends she has never met sharing your house at the same time. This puts her in an awkward position. Women are territorial to a degree. Having strange women prancing around in their panties is not a good look. The focus should be on her at all times. If she is someone you are getting to know, keep the friends, male or female, from spending the night.

4. Constantly talking about your exes or showing her photos of you with other women.

No woman wants to hear what you and your ex did, when you did it, how you did it and how it was while doing it. ONLY talk about your exes if she talks about hers OR asks you a specific question about them. And showing her photos of them? Tacky, tacky, tacky! We can do without the visuals thank you. Ask yourself, what are you trying to prove? This is never appropriate.

5. Being late picking her up from the airport.

This is by far and wide one of the greatest sins a man can commit against a woman. Whether she is visiting you, or coming home from a long trip: Always be on time. On time means being early. Show her that you care enough about her to be there when she arrives. If it is not possible, hire a car service. No one likes to be left standing alone in a strange airport wondering if anyone will show.

6. Begging her for sex/ talking about sex all the time.

Desperation is always a turn off. You want to let her know you are not pressed to get it from her. I had a friend tell me a she met a guy and on their first date he took her to a porno shop. Ok, pump the brakes! Either he is a freak looking for a Jump Off, or he has no sense of boundaries and no sense of what is or isn't appropriate. This is 'deal breaker' behavior.

7. Asking her for money.

Have your 'ish together. Never ask a woman for money—under *any* circumstances. Men are natural providers. If she thinks she will have to take care of you, this could potentially be a deal breaker.

8. Asking her to pay for your date.

Some people believe this may only be appropriate if she asks you out. Most women are old-fashioned and believe the man should pay for dates. Globally and throughout history, there are many cultures where the men have paid dowries to families for women they want to marry, and so on. This is tradition. It is considered gentlemanly for the man to treat his date to meals and so on. Historically, men are the providers. Women are attracted to men who can show, via dates that he is financially responsible and fiscally stable. But I also too believe that most men can appreciate a woman who offers to pick up the check every now and then as a show of her independence. But hey, you know the rules, so don't kill the messenger.

If you believe a woman should pay for a date, for instance, if she invites you, subtly make that clear to her upfront to avoid a potentially tense situation. The last thing you want to do is put her on the spot while you are on a date if she wasn't expecting to pay. To avoid a precarious situation, when/if she invites you, you could say: "Wow you are taking *me* out, so should I leave my wallet at home?" Or, "That's nice of you. I haven't been treated by a woman in a long time." Get it? You are conveying to her *she is paying.* She will understand it and it is in a positive, subtle way. This way, you both are clear and can avoid any misunderstandings.

9.   Blowing up her phone as soon as you get her phone number.

One word: desperation. Don't call, e-mail, text message, or IM a lady more than twice in the first week of meeting her. And do not call her after 11:00 pm. It is disrespectful, and you always want to treat a woman with what? Respect. OK, moving on.

10. Talking on your cell phone while on a date with her.

There is nothing more rude or annoying. Constantly looking at your cell, answering, and having conversations while on a date is disrespectful. Who can't turn their mobile off for an hour? Even the President takes vacations. Turn the cell off!

So you have done all those things and you want to know when can you get the nooky?

TIME LIMIT ON SEX

There should not be a time limit put on how long a woman or man should wait before they have sex. It is all about the comfort level and the dynamic between you.

A person who places a time restriction on when you can consummate the relationship appears to be too intent on controlling the situation or trying to play games. The bottom line is, there shouldn't be a restriction set before hand; but the key is, both people should be comfortable with taking the next step at the same time.

A man should never think he can convince or talk a woman into having sex with him, but rather, allow her to come to her own conclusions that she wants to give herself to him because he deserves her and it is what you each desire.

CHAPTER 9

THE SIXTH MAN:
AVOIDING THE BENCH

HOW TO AVOID THE DREADED "FRIENDS" CATEGORY

Something a man never wants to hear, "*I love you like a friend.*" How did you get put in the dreaded "friends" category? After all, you have wined and dined her, listened to all of her problems day in and day out, been there for her through thick and thin, never forgot her birthday, and have more than put your share of time in.

Now, you have patiently been waiting for her to call you up at 3 a.m. to meet at her place, as she reminds you to bring a pack of condoms and a bottle of Tequila. But in reality, you get her 3 a.m. phone call to come by, and when you arrive with your condoms and liquor, she starts to cry on your shoulder about some other guy breaking her heart! After two hours, you haven't cracked open one single condom and your balls are blue. You finally leave, but only after she has fallen asleep on you. You are confused and ultimately pissed because you couldn't even get a sympathy lay!

How do you avoid landing in this frustrating situation? There are things you can do, but I refuse to lie to you. It is not easy because she has decided whether or not she wants to sleep with you within the first five minutes of meeting you.

Here is why she may not "like you like that":

- She may not find you sexy.
- You may not be her type.
- She may already be in a relationship.
- She may deliberately not be in a relationship and does not want to date at that moment.
- The timing may not be good for her.
- You may physically remind her of someone she does not like.
- She may have the wrong impression of you.

Not to fret. The key here is this: it *is* possible that you can change her mind over time. But this is going to take some very calculated moves on your part. You must claim your territory, (**and claim** *her)* from the beginning. She must see you as the 'alpha dog.'

The truth is, if you've developed a friendship, there is obviously *something* she likes about you. This is a great foundation. The goal for you now will be to establish from the jump that you are *not* interested in being her friend. Let me say it another way: You must be willing to lose her friendship, and walk away/distance yourself, if from here on out, she does not respond to you in a romantic way.

If this happens, you may not end up with the girl of your dreams, but you will at least end up with your pride. She'll respect you for it.

The following will be your strategy if you find yourself being pushed into the "just a friend" category:

- Flirt up front
- Make it clear that you want to be more than a friend
- Don't be shy
- Give her compliments
- Be supportive but don't be a sucker
- Don't sleep together constantly without sex or affection or foreplay
- Tell her you can be friends but you want to be more. If she reacts by laughing, it's not a good sign
- Get her to talk about sex, what she likes or dislikes
- Don't let her play dress up with you
- Don't show any signs of weakness
- Don't go overboard with your helpfulness
- Don't be a mark

Don't lend her money without a promissory note if you want the money back. Some women conveniently confuse the words "loan" and "gift." They may think because you are interested in them that you want to give them things. So be clear up front on whether it is a gift or a loan.

Unless you want to give to her freely, don't let her make it a habit. Only loan or give her money once before she is in a relationship with you if you choose to at all.

You do not want to end up as an easy "mark" or feeling like you have been played if she walks away. If you can afford to and think that she has shown the signs of wanting to date you and not just be your buddy, consider your gifts as a down payment of sorts.

NEVER PAY THE:

"YOU ARE NOT MY DREAM MAN" TAX

This high tax is paid by the man she's in the relationship with who doesn't quite measure up to her "ideal" man. In other words, she's "settling." A woman who dates a man who is not her dream man, or is someone she is not totally happy with, may "tax" him. What do I mean? She will make demands on him, demands he may not be comfortable with. Demands she definitely *wouldn't* make on a man she *was* happy with! Sometimes though, the man who is taxed this way may not have a problem with it, being that this kind of dynamic usually occurs when a man is dating a woman he somehow feels is out of his league; a woman whose company he considers himself lucky to be in.

This is a no-no! Remember, <u>confidence</u>, <u>always</u>! Otherwise, the weekly shopping sprees, shiny new car, cash gifts, and once-a-month sex (if he is lucky) is the tax he will be paying until someone she likes better comes along. All relationships should be reciprocal, and a fair exchange. If your woman constantly takes from you, and you can't get a home-cooked meal, a massage, a sweet exchange of conversation, a sincere show of care and concern, leave! That is, unless you're a glutton for punishment. If so, then by all means stay with her and be emasculated at every turn. Be aware that you aren't just losing money, but you're losing her respect.

Just be warned that this expensive tax diminishes a man to a whipping boy, and is not in any way fair to him. So, don't settle for the "friend" role or pay the tax, if you value yourself and what you truly bring to the relationship. Demand more!

Chapter 10

TECHNICAL FOUL

"Ain't no p*ssy good enough to be burnt while I'm up in it." —*Snoop Dogg*

Truer words were never spoken. I would be remiss not to provide you with information that could potentially save your life. Please read through this chapter carefully. Although we sometimes make light of sex, SEX IS NO JOKE. There are hundreds of sexually transmitted diseases and choosing who to have sex with can be a life or death decision. There are diseases to consider and birth control.

Rule #1

- Never depend on a woman to provide contraception.

You must be responsible for your part in preventing pregnancies. It is possible that a woman can be 100% honest with you and be on the birth-control pill and it fails the same way condoms can break.

How many of you use baby oil as lubrication for a condom? Massage oil? Oil-based lubricants like petroleum jelly or Vaseline or even lotion? All these make condoms break!

Further, there are many women who are on the pill, and take medication such as antibiotics which greatly diminishes the effect of the pill. Question: whether or not it is possible to get pregnant while on the pill? The answer to that is, **anything is possible**. It does not have to be a woman that is trying to "set you up" to be her baby daddy who has her birth-control pill fail. She may have naïvely or innocently done something to cause the pill not to be as effective. Therefore, look out for **you** first.

My suggestion is simple:

Do not sleep with anyone you wouldn't choose to have a child with.

This may seem extreme, but *anything* is possible. The Brothers who are out there with the crazy baby mama drama from some woman they just met a few times, or a few hours, all know exactly what I mean. The pleasure is not worth the risk.

After a woman gets pregnant, it is ultimately her decision how she wants to handle her pregnancy. For you, it is too late to turn back time. The preventative measures must be paramount and practiced each and every time. You have to be serious about your life and take full responsibility for your actions and that starts long before the panties drop.

CHOOSING A CONDOM

A latex condom is best at preventing diseases and pregnancies. However, before purchasing, you may want to consider the following information:

- Condoms break.

Any condom can break during intercourse, for many different reasons. Breakage is almost invariably the result of improper handling, such as using teeth to open the foil or keeping condoms in wallets or car glove boxes where heat will eventually break down the latex in the condom. Always check the expiration date.

- Most men who break condoms do not use them properly.

A lubricant must be WATER-based, and most lotions contain some form of oil. Oil is a latex condom's #1 enemy because it immediately begins to erode the latex. Do not use lotion or baby oil or hair grease because it is convenient. Use a water-based lubricant intended for this purpose, such as Astroglide, Sensura, or Liquid Silk.

- A lot of men try to use the excuse that condoms don't feel as good as the real thing.

Well how does peeing fire feel? How do herpes blisters feel? How does seeing crabs jump off your body and genital region or crawl around in your bed feel? How does death feel? I thought so. It's a matter of safety. Life and death. Get tested and wait six months to make sure you're both healthy. Make sure that during this period, you have had no risk factors or sex with anyone else. Then, get tested a second time. You will be clear to use other methods of birth control.

- Most regular size condoms can fit over the forearm of a woman.

So unless you are part of a circus act, you can find a condom that fits you.

For those gentlemen who have thick, broad penises, AKA the Mandingos, there are condoms specifically manufactured for you. Magnums are the Rapper's condom of choice. They so readily brag about tearing them open in their songs. These larger than average men find regular condoms fit too snugly. There are three large-size condoms available, Magnum and Trojan-Enz and Pleasure Plus. Obviously most rappers prefer the Magnum because of its 'for big boys only' reputation. The Pleasure Plus condom has a baggier head that allows for more friction and stimulation. Although, a similar sensation can be achieved with a regular condom. Just put a pea size dollop of lubricant into the end of the condom before putting it on.

Note: You can still get Herpes and HPV from the skin not protected by a condom.

➢ Spermicides should be used only in addition to condoms, never in place of them.

➢ Don't buy "novelty" condoms, such as "glow-in-the-dark." These are not intended to provide pregnancy or STD protection.

➢ If you're shy about purchasing condoms, get over it. You are being responsible. But if you must, buy them online.

If the relationship becomes monogamous and you want to have unprotected sex, you both have to go and get an HIV/STD test **together**. It's not very romantic, but at the least you know you are both "clean" and free of any potentially deadly or incurable diseases.

THE DISEASES

The following is a list of the most common sexually transmitted diseases along with their symptoms, potential dangers, and treatments and/or cures. There are currently over 50 known STDs! So this is a **short list** of the most common and/or rapidly spread. Always ask for a FULL screening of every STD when getting tested. Never self-diagnose when it comes to personal health. Many of these symptoms can be caused by factors other than an STD, and many STDs can exist for a very long time before any symptoms are even noticeable. If you think you have an STD, **run** to see your doctor. Better safe than sorry. There are also a number of free clinics in every area. So, there is no excuse to be trifling.

If your physician confirms your suspicions, follow the medication instructions until finished. Most people stop when there symptoms go away, but that doesn't mean you are healed. You also must tell your partner(s) immediately. There is no question that breaking the news can be difficult and awkward. But she needs to know for her own health in order to get treated, and so she doesn't potentially re-infect you.

CHLAMYDIA

What is chlamydia?
Chlamydia (klah MIH dee ah) is the most common and most invisible sexually transmitted *bacterial* infection in the United States. It is a kind of bacteria that can infect the penis, vagina, cervix, anus, urethra, eye, or throat.

What are the symptoms of chlamydia?

Usually, there are no symptoms. Seventy-five percent of women and 50 percent of men with chlamydia have no symptoms. Most people are not aware that they have the infection.

When <u>men</u> have symptoms, they may experience:

- pain or burning feeling while urinating
- pus or watery or milky discharge from the penis
- swollen or tender testicles
- rectal inflammation

When women have symptoms, they may experience:

- abdominal pain
- abnormal vaginal discharge
- bleeding between menstrual periods
- cervical or rectal inflammation
- low-grade fever
- mucopurulent cervicitis (MPC) — a yellowish discharge from the cervix that may have a foul odor
- vaginal bleeding after intercourse
- painful intercourse
- painful urination
- the urge to urinate more than usual

Men often don't take these symptoms seriously because the symptoms may appear only early in the day and can be very mild.

How is chlamydia spread?

- Vaginal and anal intercourse
- a woman to her fetus during birth
- hand to the eye and during oral sex

Is there a cure?

Yes. Chlamydia is easy to treat. Various antibiotics kill chlamydia bacteria. Both partners must be treated before having sex again to avoid re-infection after treatment. Some clinicians will provide their patients with medications to take home to their partner. Follow-up testing three to four months after treatment may be suggested.

GONORRHEA

Known as "the clap," gonorrhea is often thought of old news. However, the disease is still rampant in our country today. Similar to Chlamydia, it is a bacterial infection that can be completely asymptomatic, meaning no symptoms at all. In men, the symptoms can include a yellow puss-like discharge from the penis, pain while urinating, the need to urinate often, and pain in the lower abdomen. In women it often goes undetected until permanent damage has already occurred, like sterility, tubal pregnancies, and chronic pain. **This STD is highly contagious and can be spread through any contact with the penis, vulva area, mouth, or anus without penetration.**

The good news is that if detected early, gonorrhea is easily curable with antibiotics.

101

HPV

What is HPV?

HPV stands for Human Papilloma Virus. There are more than 100 types of HPV. Some types produce warts — that affect the genital sex organs.

- HPV is a common virus. There are 40 types of it that are sexually transmitted.
- A few types of HPV can persist and cause cervical cancer.
- There is a vaccine to prevent two of the types that cause 70 percent of the cases of cervical cancer in women.

About 40 types of HPV can infect the genital area — the vulva, vagina, cervix, rectum, anus, penis, or scrotum.

- Some types may cause genital warts. These are called low-risk types.
- Some types may cause cell changes that sometimes lead to cervical and certain other genital and throat cancers. These are called high-risk types. They do not usually have visible symptoms.
- Most types seem to have no harmful effect at all.

Certain forms of HPV cause visible **genital warts**, though some strains cause no warts at all. Genital warts are growths that appear on the penis, scrotum, groin, or thigh. They can be raised or flat, single or multiple, small or large. All sexually active men and women are susceptible to contracting HPV. It is spread by direct contact during vaginal, oral, or anal sex with someone who has the virus.

In women they can be on the external or internal genitals, and though rare, infants can be infected during childbirth.

Genital warts can be treated in several ways, including freezing, laser surgery, and topical creams. **None are cures.** The strains of HPV that don't produce genital warts usually go undetected until a woman has an abnormality in her Pap smear. Genital HPV is manageable with proper diagnosis.

Because HPV is a virus that can lie dormant for years, you may suddenly have an outbreak after being monogamous for years. You usually have to specifically ask for this test when getting a check up. Men need to check themselves regularly, and look for any growths on the skin, which even if painless, should be discussed with your doctor.

There is a new vaccine called Gardasil recently approved by the FDA recommended for girls ages 13-26 and as young as 9. Please consult your physician for more information on preventing this disease.

SYPHILIS

Syphilis is a very dangerous bacterial infection, and an estimated 104,000 new cases in men and women will be contracted in the United States this year. If left untreated, syphilis can be fatal and/or cause irreparable damage to the heart, brain, eyes, and joints.

- Forty percent of all babies born to mothers with syphilis die during childbirth or are born with abnormalities.

Symptoms are painless sores, rashes on the palms and feet, swollen lymph nodes. This disease is highly contagious through oral, vaginal, and anal sex, as well as through open wounds on the skin. When detected early, syphilis is curable with strong doses of antibiotics.

HERPES

It is estimated that somewhere between 200,000 and 500,000 new cases of genital herpes will be contracted this year and that 45 million Americans are infected already. Even more frightening is the number of people who don't know they are infected.

There are two viruses that cause genital herpes:

Herpes Simplex 1, which occurs orally, and **Herpes Simplex 2**, which occurs genitally.

Herpes Simplex 1 is typically what we refer to as cold sores on, around, or inside the lips and mouth. YOU CAN NOT GET RID OF HERPES. The visible symptoms of herpes simplex 2 include itchy bumps or tiny blisters on the genital area of men, typically on the shaft of the penis, at the end of the foreskin or near the head of the penis.
In women the outbreak occurs near or inside the vagina and labia or rectum. Men can also get herpes near the anus, even if they have never had anal intercourse. Sometimes herpes lesions first appear in areas related to the genitals by nerve endings but not actually on the genitals. In this case, the buttocks and thighs are common.

- If you or your lady have visible cold sores on your mouth, never receive or give oral sex, as you can transmit herpes simplex 1 to genitally. Then you will have Herpes 1 and 2.

Herpes can be contracted on any area of skin or mucous membrane, depending upon what area was in intimate contact with a lesion. The first outbreak of genital herpes may last between twelve and fourteen days, and is typically the most severe, while subsequent outbreaks are shorter in duration (four to five days) and milder. Mostly, people with herpes never get this first bad episode and just start out with a mild, or asymptomatic infection.

Herpes is highly contagious during an outbreak, but it can also be contagious when the virus **appears** to be dormant. This is because it can reactivate without symptoms in most people with herpes.

The key is to get any inflammation of the skin, or blister, or chafed area checked out while you can still see it. However, if you think you have been exposed to herpes, only the Western blot blood test can make the diagnosis without symptoms.

Yes, it's hard to tell someone you are not perfect, especially in a new relationship. But you must inform your partner! I have a friend with Herpes and she has had numerous partners and with <u>unprotected sex</u>.

> **She is a pretty girl and just because someone is pretty, does not mean they don't have diseases.**

At the time of sexual intercourse, she never told ANY of her partners she was infected, even though she knew she had a moral obligation to disclose it. But the men never asked her, either. Maybe, if they had, she may have felt more compelled to tell them. The problem here again is that you are leaving your health status up to someone else. Get tested. Use a condom at the very least. Ask the hard questions.

There is no cure for this virus, though the oral medications have proved to be highly successful in both minimizing the symptoms of current outbreaks and suppressing recurrences.

If you and your partner are working on getting pregnant, and you have herpes and your partner does not, it is paramount for you to use proper safer sex practices during the pregnancy and consider suppressive antiviral treatment.

HEPATITIS B

Infection caused by the hepatitis B virus is not usually considered an STD; however, it is spread through infected semen, vaginal secretions, and saliva, and it is 100 times more infectious than HIV. You can get hepatitis B from vaginal, oral, or – especially – anal sex. You can also get infected with the virus through direct contact with an infected person via open sores or cuts. This means that if someone in your home is infected, you can contract hepatitis B by using the same razor or toothbrush.

Hepatitis B attacks the liver. Some carriers develop cirrhosis and/or liver cancer. Your chances of contracting liver cancer are 200 times higher if you're a hepatitis B carrier. Symptoms, when they appear, can be very much like those of the stomach flu. See your doctor immediately if you have nausea, unexplainable fatigue, dark urine, and/or yellowing of the eyes and skin. New, effective, and safe treatments are now available. However, the vast majority of people who get hepatitis B as adults, recover on their own.

There is a vaccination for hepatitis B. It is a series of shots, given in the arm. You must have all three shots to be safe. The vaccine will protect you after you have completed the shots from any potential risk, but you should have a test to make sure you responded. This, and the HPV vaccine for young girls, is the only STD vaccine that works and is widely available.

- Hepatitis B mainly attacks young men and women in their teens and twenties.

Once you contract it, you have a small chance of becoming a carrier for life or even getting chronic liver problems or cancer. Ask for your vaccination—especially if you are someone who is changing partners frequently.

AIDS/HIV

AIDS is the number one cause of death for African-Americans between the ages of 25 and 44. AND THE NUMBER ONE CAUSE OF DEATH OF AFRICAN AMERICAN WOMEN. This is not a joke. You can get it. Period. AIDS does not have a face and if it did, it could look just like mine or yours.

An estimated two thirds of new cases come from people who were unaware that they were infected. Black women account for 72% of all the new HIV cases and 67% of Black women with HIV contracted it from heterosexual sex. African-American women are 23 times more likely to be infected with AIDS than white women. African-American men are almost nine times more likely to be infected with AIDS than white men. Based on the staggering statistics from the Centers for Disease Control and Prevention, you have every reason to be concerned.

How can you get HIV?

HIV is transmitted in blood, semen, vaginal fluids, and breast milk. The most common ways HIV is spread are by:

- having unprotected sexual intercourse with someone who has the virus
- sharing needles or syringes with someone who has the virus
- being deeply punctured with a needle or surgical instrument contaminated with the virus
- getting HIV-infected blood, semen, or vaginal secretions into open wounds or sores

HIV and AIDS are not the same thing. One is the precursor of the other. Acquired Immune Deficiency Syndrome (AIDS) is a diagnosis resulting from infection with a virus known as the Human Immunodeficiency Virus (HIV). When someone tests positive for HIV, his or her system has been exposed to the virus and his/her body is presenting an immune response to it.

There are usually no symptoms accompanying HIV. People can get the virus and feel terrific for many years. Left untreated, the virus almost always leads to AIDS, and because it is the immune system that fails, the symptoms for AIDS can look like anything from a cold to cancer.

Although there is no cure for AIDS, there are new drugs that slow the effect HIV has on the immune system. It can take up to six months for one's immune system to show antibodies, which means that you have tested positive for exposure. Every sexually active man and woman should have two HIV tests – one after risky behavior and another after waiting six months. The six-month waiting period will ensure a clean bill of health before having unprotected sex with any new partner. Sadly, in this day and age, it isn't always enough to accept a verbal declaration of good health. Many, many people have been deceived by lovers who claimed to be HIV negative and weren't.

It is very important that you ask to see the results of your lover's HIV test and all tests of sexually transmitted diseases, especially in the case of (but not limited to) women you don't know well. Please, for your own safety and peace of mind, go together to get tested. It is also important that she see your test results. If your lover refuses to show you her test results, avoid having unprotected sex with her at all. Remember, she is being secretive about something that affects *your* health and quite possibly your life. No one should want to keep her/his good health a secret.

In closing, I want to leave you with some real points on HIV/AIDS:

#1: There are several types (or clades) of the HIV virus and strains: So even if a man or a woman is already positive, he or she can still become infected by another form of the virus and is even more susceptible, given the weakened state of the immune system.

#2: "HIV positive" means you have been exposed to the virus that causes AIDS. Your body shows a positive immune response to HIV.

#3: Wait six months after risky behavior before getting tested. This is because **it can take up to six months for antibodies to show up in a test,** although most people (95 percent) test positive within three months of exposure, using the antibodies testing methods.

#4: Just because someone has no detectable viral load, as the Magic Johnson rumors once stated, does not mean he or she cannot infect someone else or has cured themselves of the virus. There is no cure.

#5: Most people who are HIV positive do not know they are infected because they have never been tested.

There are more than fifty known STDs to date

Providing you with knowledge about them is not meant to scare you, but rather to empower you. No one should have to be frightened into taking control of his or her sexual health. Rather, with this information hopefully being safe and careful becomes a matter of self-respect. Without protection, there just isn't an excuse good enough to participate in a sexual relationship with someone whose health you're not 100 percent sure about. It's absolutely your responsibility to be honest about your health status and communicate this to your partner, no matter how casual or close your relationship. It's also your responsibility to make sure you are not passing a disease on to a lover.

Safety is essential, but it doesn't have to undermine the sensuality of your lovemaking. Be aware of all the risks and take preventative measures. The following is a list of resources you can contact for further information.

RESOURCES

Centers for Disease Control and Prevention (commonly known as the CDC) www.cdc.gov

Public Health Service AIDS Hotline
800-342-AIDS (24 hours a day, 7 days a week)

STD National Hotline (Centers for Disease Control)
800-227-8922 (8:00 A.M. – 11:00 P.M. EST weekdays)
www.ashastd.org

Hepatitis Hotline
888-443-7232

National Herpes Hotline
919-361-8488

ABOUT SEXUALITY

American Association of Sex Educators, Counselors and Therapists (AASECT)
P.O. Box 238
Mt. Vernon, Iowa 52314
www.AASECT.org

Society for the Scientific Study of Sexuality (AKA the 4Ss)
www.sscwisc.edu/ssss

Sex Information Education Council of the United States (SEICUS)
212-819-9770

PLANNED PARENTHOOD
www.plannedparenthood.org
Clinics are found throughout the States

*All citations are from the CDC. At the time we compiled the information from the Center for Disease Control (CDC) and Planned Parenthood in this chapter, the statistics were up-to-date. If you would like more information or current statistics, on all known STDs and communicable diseases, visit each website.

CHAPTER 11

TOUCHDOWN

Bumping uglies, humping, doing the nasty, getting down, knocking boots, cutting, doing it, smashing, hooking up, getting it, freakin', banging, coitis, A.K.A. **S-E-X.** Do I have your attention?

Statistics say most men think about sex every 52 seconds. It is no wonder that every where you turn, you are being sold sex. Take a look at this book cover. You are being sold sex. So now that we understand that it is a part of our every day life, we can address the issues that lie before us when it comes to what men and women desire from sex. I do not believe all men just want to hit it, split it and quit it. Some do, there is no doubt about it. But I want to hold on to the delusion that most men care about the women they are sleeping with and want to please them. The problem is, most men want to please women, but most women are not getting pleased. Sorry, but it is true.

LIES YOUR BROTHER TOLD YOU

Not every technique works on every woman. Some women like a lot of foreplay, or for their nipples to be pinched while you stroke her hair. Others may not like intercourse very often and prefer oral sex. There is no universal rule to pleasing women. Just as our sexual appetites vary so do our attitudes regarding sex. Men think women can only have sex with men if they are in love with them. Not true. Some women like sex just for the pure pleasure of it and can detach from their emotions just as easily as men. Not all women "catch feelings" after sex. Some women are natural explorers and don't mind elicit or taboo sexual experimentation such as participating in orgies. Some may label that behavior as "ho-ish." Or, maybe this kind of girl insists that sleeping with all your boys is natural. Some women who sleep with both sexes, do not necessarily consider themselves lesbians. While some say they are just sexually free and don't mind munching carpet for variety or sport. So there is no global one rule or collective label when it comes to sex. To each his own.

WHAT TURNS A MAN ON -vs- WHAT TURNS A WOMAN ON

It doesn't take much to turn a man on. Most men are more right brain or visually oriented and are turned on by what they see. Others are turned on with a good, stiff wind or warm water flowing over their member in the shower. It doesn't take much. Men almost instinctively know how to pleasure themselves. Masturbation has probably become the universal male pastime. Married, gay, straight; the trend doesn't discriminate, they go at it alone—pun intended. More than likely, they learned how to pleasure themselves by accident.

After having experienced the feeling of auto stimulation, they could never go back. Often whenever the mood hits a man, and there is no woman present, he does not hesitate to entertain himself with a jerk or two or three... you get it.

According to a recent Glamour magazine survey 89% of men masturbate.

What and whom they think about during masturbation?

- 41% their wife or girlfriend
- 31% female friends or women they know
- 14% Porn Stars
- 7% Celebrities
- 7% Miscellaneous women or a composite woman

How often?

Single men do it as much as 3-4 times a week, and married or involved men as much as 3-4 times per week. Men can do it quickly and efficiently and everywhere imaginable from the office, the beach, the airplane, and even in their cars while driving. This brings a whole new meaning to safe sex.

SEX IS JUST SEX

Because men are so autonomous, even when it comes to sex, they can become more aloof and removed with their partner. Some men disconnect during sex and never see a woman for the sensuous and loving creature she is. These men look at women and only see an A.T.M.—Ass, Titties, and Mouth. Other men see a woman's body as a reciprocal playground. Wherever you happen to fall in that paradigm, most men fall short in pleasing her. And I'm not talking about a lack of inches.

MOST MEN HAVE PAID FOR SEX AT LEAST ONCE

It is easy for a man to connect sexually to a woman but disconnect emotionally. They are capable of having no strings attached sex which is why most men have paid for sex or had sex with a professional working girl at least once in their lives. If a woman asks a man if he has, he will most certainly lie about it. But I assure you that most have. Think Hugh Grant or your daring trips to Las Vegas where prostitution is legal. Most of the sexual tourism in Brazil is from African-American men who travel there to pay for cheap sex with the world's most beautiful prostitutes.

These men have no problem going to strip clubs and paying to see naked women or paying them for sexual favors. Paying is open to interpretation depending on whom you ask. Some men feel a date consisting of an expensive meal or a present he may purchase, or a bill he may pay, as a subtle, yet, arguable means of paying for sex. The latter is highly insulting to most women. So if you agree with this line of thinking, I suggest keeping those sexist feelings on the down low.

HOW OFTEN YOU ARE NOT PLEASING HER

Women fake orgasms 85% of the time

Well since I brought it up…

WHAT IS AN ORGASM?

An orgasm can be described as rhythmic muscular contractions of the genitals (sex organs) combined with waves of intense pleasurable sensations. In males, it results in the ejaculation of semen. An orgasm usually "comes" or happens at the height of sexual arousal when the peak of sexual stimulation occurs, causing a "climax" which results in a release of sexual tensions.

Orgasms in women vary and are a result of physiological as well as psychological factors. In women, it is a rush of emotion and physical enjoyment and a release of many kinds. Many women can have a series of orgasms, or multiple orgasms, one following shortly after another. Because of the sudden and unexpected release of our hormones, women often cry after sex, something that completely turns men off. Some women may laugh or cry or feel a complete sense of euphoria. We all have different reactions to this release at different times.

WHY WOMEN FAKE ORGASMS

When I had this discussion regarding how often a woman fakes orgasms at a table full of men, all of them with egos bigger than life, each one of them thought that they were never lied to when it came to their woman or partners having an orgasm. They all said, "I know when I'm putting in work." And, "I know when I've done my job." I loved the, "I know if I blew her back out." When the other women finally arrived, I asked them how many times they were satisfied out of ten sexual encounters. The overwhelming answer was a mere **three**.

So, just because you "beat it up" or made her scream loud enough that all the neighbors could hear, or because she

117

dug track marks into your back when you laid the pipe that night, does not mean you made her *come*.

Men have tremendous egos. If women don't know a single thing about a man, we know this to be self-evident. The honest truth is we fake orgasms 99% of the time because we do not want to hurt your feelings. If you are a man we care for and we know you are trying your best to give us pleasure, and an orgasm for us does not happen, you will inevitably feel as if you failed and that we were not satisfied. You would further incorrectly think you were a horrible lover and perhaps no good in bed or at least not during that instance.

What men do not understand is that a woman does not have to have an orgasm to be satisfied. If the intimacy was there, the connection was there, and the lovemaking was brilliant on your part, that all adds up to great sex for us. A man who is a good lover will work hard to prevent himself from having an orgasm first so his woman can have hers first. But men focus so much on the *results* that they can sometimes lose sight of the goal, which is to make love to physically demonstrate how he feels for his partner.

SOME WOMEN HAVE NEVER HAD AN ORGASM

In fact, 15% percent of women have never had an orgasm. But this does not mean that she has not had great sex. Sometimes there could be a physical reason that will prevent a woman from having an orgasm. The bottom line is, though, a woman can climax without achieving orgasm. Because your egos are so fragile, we don't always tell you the truth when it comes to the big O.

HOW DO YOU KNOW IF YOU ARE PLEASING HER

We know that a man ejaculates sperm when he "comes" but exactly what does a woman do? The answer is it depends on the woman. A small percentage of women ejaculate a fluid, which is not urine, from their urethras during orgasm, but most women do not. Typically, there is no physical evidence of orgasm, because she erupts and contracts from the *inside.* You know if you are pleasing her because you have to look for the signs. This applies to anything with women. Check her body language.

Whether you are going down on her, massaging her breasts, or licking her inner thigh, you should look for the signs from her that tell you if she likes it or if she doesn't. It's always a good idea to talk. Talking during sex can be very sexy and arousing. If you are kissing her neck and you gently lift her hair and bite her neck ever so gently, she will respond by breathing heavier, or pulling away. Common sense should tell you if she pulls away, she probably did not like it. But if she moans, you know to continue doing what you are doing. The signs are always there unless you have a woman who is stiff in the bed and just lays there without ever saying or doing anything. I hope for your sake that you don't get that 'cold fish' type of performance. But nine-times-out-of-ten, she will let you know with a nonverbal form of communication.

If you refuse to pay attention to your partner's signs during sex and go for broke with your "patented moves" that you think turns every single woman on, then there is absolutely no hope for you.

No two vaginas are created equal. There is nothing more irritating than a man who already thinks he knows what you will like, and no matter what you say or do to convince him otherwise, he has a plan and he is going to stick to it. For instance, one thing I cannot stand is a man to tickle my feet. Caressing, touching, licking, sucking, that is different. But if you try to tickle my feet, you might get kicked in the teeth. The funny thing is, if a man tries to tickle my feet and I immediately withdraw them and my mood changes and I give him a stern look and firmly say, "I do not like my feet to be tickled please don't do that," and homeboy still insists on tickling my feet, he kills the mood for the rest of the night. You always want to read the obvious signs. *Obvious* meaning she tells you she doesn't like it! You may think it's cute at first, but it is not cute when she suddenly blows out the candles and puts on her biggest grandma panties and tells you that you have to leave because she has to wash her hair.

WHAT IS A G-SPOT?

The G-spot, or less commonly known as the Grafenberg spot, named after the scientist who discovered and coined the term, is the area just inside the front wall of the vagina (the stomach side) usually between 11 and 2 o'clock, that when stimulated, feels like a smooth but firm rubber ball about the size of a dime or pea. This spot or cluster of nerves swells when it is excited to about the size of a quarter and is widely believed to be the equivalent of a man's prostate gland. Which, also when stimulated, can cause a man to ejaculate without ever touching his penis. The G-spot stimulation is widely agreed to be the source of vaginal orgasms versus clitoral orgasms. Vaginal orgasms result from penetration of the vagina.

Clitoral orgasms result from direct stimulation of the clitoris. Most times it's either or for a woman, and sometimes she can climax using both forms of stimuli.

HOW WAS IT? HOW TO GET THE REAL TRUTH FROM HER

> **The worst thing from a man's perspective that women do if they are not being pleased is to withhold this information from him**

Most men say they prefer a woman to talk about what she likes and to show him what she likes. Some women do this by simply moving a certain way or by taking his hand and placing it where she wants to be touched. Some women are naturally good at teaching without saying a word. And most men who are paying attention remember what she likes and what she doesn't like simply by how she reacts to what he is doing. If she is moaning and grabbing the sheets when you do a certain move, then that is usually a pretty good sign. But if she is thumbing her fingers against the wall and looking at the clock, chances are, she is bored to tears.

Have you ever been in an argument with someone and she blurts out how you don't please her in bed? You are not alone. Most women do not know how to broach the subject of not being satisfied, so the majority of the time it is never addressed. A man usually wants to please his woman partially because of his ego. Some who are not really into their partner only do the minimal amount to please her. But the man who *wants* to rock his girl's world, suffers by her silence. She does more damage than good by not speaking up.

Everything is in the *approach*. It's not <u>what</u> you say, but <u>how</u> you say something that is key. You can start the conversation by telling her how much you enjoy a certain move she does. Then, you can ask her what she likes. By using this reverse psychology, she may be compelled to ask you what she could do better to please you. Most men would more than likely say more BJs, less teeth, and less talking. Women might say more tongue, more hands, and more intimacy. You will be surprised at what she might reveal. Maybe she likes it rough or wants you to role-play. Maybe she wants to fulfill your ultimate fantasy or invite her best friend to bed. So, gently bring it up first.

WHAT WOMEN REALLY WANT

Women in general are more romantic, idealistic and fantasy oriented in love and in relationships. Yes, we read romance novels, and cry during commercials, and get choked up watching weddings on TV. We love a fairy tale and a good-girl-gets-the-guy love story.

WOMEN WANT INTIMACY

We want the connection. We want the bond. We want the intimacy. Pleasure can be derived from intimacy. We briefly touched on this in the first chapter. A way to a woman's heart is through her mind. If she feels safe, it means she trusts you. You must be intimate with her long before ever touching her. Sharing, caring and bearing your heart and true feelings are all forms of intimacy. This is what we wholeheartedly desire. Once that is achieved, she is more than willing to give her body to you and will be willing to pleasure you.

In order to satisfy a woman you must first understand her psyche and then her body and how it works. Many women don't even know their own bodies. But here is a diagram to help you identify the correct parts:

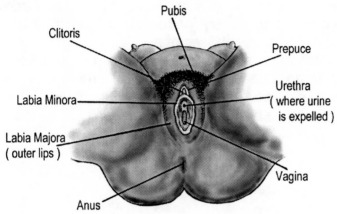

No two vaginas are created equal. A vagina is like a flower with hundreds of different varieties. They all look different. They are beautiful and delicate and need care and attention. They have different colors, buds, scents, roots, aromas, pubic hair, clitoris' and shapes. The variety is what is exciting to see. In terms of looks, some vagina's inner labia also known as the labia minora, (small lips) extend well beyond her outer labia. Some women have larger labia or "fat lips" which often make men more aroused when viewing or pressing against.

Men have many preferences on how he likes a woman to look, including her pubic hair.

There are countless ways a woman grooms her V section and the male's preference for what he fancies is vast. Whether it is bald, Brazilian, Charlie Chaplin, Playboy, a landing strip, regular bikini, special designs, etc. I had a friend tell me his girlfriend cut a heart shape into her pubic hair for Valentine's Day. After seeing the intricate design, he thought she was crazy for doing it and quickly left her. I thought is was a sweet gesture.

Internally speaking, a woman's reproductive system is an extension of her vagina and is often what she feels "contract" when having an orgasm. Here is what our reproductive system looks like internally:

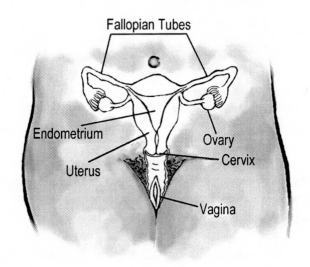

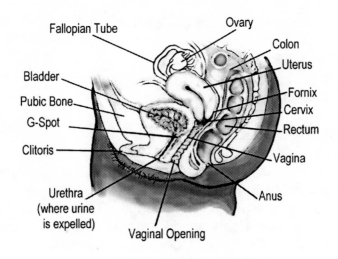

A WOMAN'S PHYSICAL PREFERENCE

> Our number one physical concern is a man's penis size
> and sometimes shape.

A close friend of mine laughs about his penis size, or lack thereof, sighting the only way he can make a woman scream during sex is if he is banging her head against the wall. Men who brag about their penis size is a big turn off. I once had a friend boast to me about being "hung like a horse." After seeing the goods, he turned out to be hung like a pony *at best*. A very nice package indeed, but he was putting a little too much on it. To my point, we all have our own idea of what 'big" is. There is no agreed upon size chart per se to measure. Maybe my barometer for a large penis was much higher than his.

DOES SIZE MATTER?

Let me think.....

Still thinking...

Ummm, ok...HELL YES!

The size of a man's penis is related to a woman's enjoyment in most cases. When people speak of penis size, they typically refer to length. Thus, a man with a short but wide penis would probably think of himself as having a small penis. Does width contribute to female sexual satisfaction? Is length more important? Width is part of size, although usually not acknowledged as "big." It is true that the vagina adapts to fit the size of the penis. Because of this vaginal adaptation, it can adjust to a penis small or large. So, despite the worries of many males about the size of their penis, <u>one vagina fits all</u>.

However, present studies were conducted to see if female college students would report their sexual satisfaction related to penis length, width, or neither.

The study polled female students who ranged in age from 18 to 25 years old. In person or via telephone, the females were asked, "In having sex, which feels better, <u>length</u> of penis or <u>width</u> of penis?"

Conclusion:

> **Women reported that penis width was more important for their sexual satisfaction than penis length.**

From the study, what women agree on that they prefer is **girth,** or **thickness,** as opposed to length.

We'd prefer a man with a sizable girth over a man's penis that is super long and "thin." The man with girth hits more nerve endings with less friction and far less effort. Again, the women have had their say. Just because a man is "long" (I'd say long in my opinion is over 7 inches), greater than average (average being about 2 inches across), **width is what we prefer** and what gives us greater pleasure. But keep in mind, what is also a turn on, is if you are happy with your size and unafraid to show it.

AVERAGE SIZE OF A MAN'S PENIS

The size of the man has nothing to do with the size of his best friend. A guy who is 5'2" could be toting a lethal weapon, and a man 6'8" could have a pencil pecker. **Therefore, the size of the man is no correlation to penis size.** But how long should it be when it's erect? Some men are show-ers and some men are grow-ers. A man's penis increases in size up to 300%. There is no standard for an erection. It differs from man to man. The man whose non-erect organ is smallish will usually achieve about 100 percent increase in length during sexual excitement, while the man whose limp penis is on the largish size will probably only manage about a 75 percent increase. In round figures, this means that the great majority of men measure between 6" and 7" in the erect position, with the average size being about 6.5".

So you can see that even if a man genuinely has got and organ that is small when he's in the non-erect state, he's also got a built in compensating factor that will probably bring him up to, or not far off, the same size as the guy he sees in the locker room who appears to be vastly "better equipped" sexually when flaccid. So, no need to sweat the *small* stuff. (I just can't help myself!).

AVERAGE SIZE OF A WOMAN'S VAGINA

The vagina of a woman who hasn't had a child is only a mere 3" long when she's not sexually excited. The figures for women who have had babies are only slightly different. And even when she has been aroused, her vagina usually extends only to a length of about 4." So it's obvious that any man's penis will fill her vagina completely, unless, of course, he happens to be one of those rare guys with an erect penile length of less than 4".

You're probably wondering how on earth a man with an average length penis of 6½" manages to insert his penis into a normal woman's vagina at all. Well, I'll tell you the answer is quite simple. The vagina has the most remarkable capacity for lengthening if something is introduced into it gradually. So the exceptional man whose penis is, say, 9" long, the AKA *"the man,"* can still make love to literally any woman, providing he excites her properly and introduces his organ very slowly. If he does this, her vagina will quite happily lengthen by 150 percent or even 200 percent to accommodate him.

Not to worry. Work whatever you have and be a master at what you do best. Never stop trying to find ways to please her body. For those with 'short comings', there are some sexual positions that decrease the length of the vagina. A few are:

- Rear entry (doggy style). The farther down her head is to the bead, the shorter the vagina becomes. If her legs are closed it allows for even more friction.

128

- Woman on her back with her feet on his shoulders. The more flexible she is the better because the closer you get to her face, her body contorts making the vagina take on a smaller "u" curve.

WHEN A WOMAN MAKES SEX BAD

OUR INSECURITIES ABOUT OUR BODIES

Our body image is the mental picture we have of ourselves. Chances are, a woman's picture of herself is a little distorted. We too often see ourselves as too tall, too short, too fat and too flat-chested. We look into the mirror and see noses that are too wide, hair that is too kinky or short, and thighs that are too jiggly. Body image problems and obsessions with weight loss, hard bodies, and breast implants are commonplace.

We are not going to mention the constant images of the 38-22-42 video girls, and rappers who have made them popular. We often see our men slobbering over photographs in magazines like Maxim or King that show women damn near butt-ass-naked and almost always bent over in a "ready-to-mount-me" position. It is no wonder that if we do not look like those impossibly fantastic looking women, then we feel, in the words of TLC, "unpretty".

Young girls are particularly vulnerable to these images. They emulate the half-naked video girls by walking around in skimpy and often see-through outfits for the entire world to see. They call "fashion" wearing miniskirts and shorts so tiny that their booty cheeks hang out the bottom.

Some men are so obsessed with giant behinds and large breasts they even ask their girlfriends to get breast implants. Personally, any man who would ask such a thing should be dropped in a large hole and burned. You don't see us asking you to go see Dr. Nip Tuck because you do not have a 10 inch penis. We don't ask men to run to the doctor to get your love handles sucked out or the tire around your gut removed. For the less shallow women, which most of us are, we do not mind the imperfections. We love you for who you are and the way you make us feel.

It's tough for women to be happy with ourselves "as is" when everywhere we look we see picture-perfect models and movie stars smiling back at us from magazine covers. Most of those images are of women who have had multiple, cosmetic surgeries, access to the best doctors and costly procedures to fix their "imperfections."

What people don't know is that photographers and movie cameras use special lenses to hide flaws and then fix the photographs to complete the <u>illusion of perfection</u>. The bottom line is, it is all smoke and mirrors. None of it is real. But that is what we are comparing ourselves to—an image.

But because men drool over these perfect looking models and video girls, we compare ourselves to those perfectly retouched women. If a woman is made to feel inferior and flawed, she may be inhibited from fully celebrating her own beauty, and could inhibit her sexually as well.

The following are just a few things that we might be insecure about when it comes to our body image…

WOMEN MAY BE INSECURE ABOUT

- a C-Section Scar from having children
- Stretch Marks
- Scars
- Weaves
- Wigs
- Fat
- Cellulite
- Small or sagging breasts

Most men already know the routine about a woman's hair, especially a Black woman's hair. What is so beautiful about us is we love to change our looks. The hair care industry is a multi-billion dollar industry. I have friends who change their hair every week. One week it might be braids, the next week a pony tail, the next week twists, and the week after a blonde weave. These types of women do not mind that you notice the changes.

And then there are other women who wear extensions or weaves that might want you to think that their hair is all natural.

Unless she has specifically told you she is wearing hair extensions (weave), keep your hands away from her hair!

I say this so you can avoid a potentially embarrassing situation for her. If her hair is long, you can move her hair or touch her hair at the bottom, so as not to disturb anything she might have going on near her scalp,

131

which is where you can tell if a woman has anything artificially added.

As beautiful as a birth of a baby might be, the residual effects are anything but to the mother. No one particularly likes or wants stretch marks, sagging breasts, or C-section scars. I once had a very well known sex symbol rapper express that he liked a little bit of sagging breasts and a slightly soft belly. Needless to say the women at the table loved him even more for feeling that way and going against the grain and keeping it real. He did not desire perfection and he found the beauty in what most women consider as flaws.

To that point, if you happen to be in an intimate setting with a woman and you notice the imperfections, pay more attention to what you like about her body and make sure you let her know it. You can say you love her hips or the curve of her back. Maybe she has extraordinary feet, flawless skin or astonishing nipples that make you want to slap your mama. Whatever you like most about her physically, make sure you specifically express it to her and show her when you are making love.

BEING ON HER PERIOD

If a woman is on her menstrual cycle, or period, she may not feel as confident about having sex or want to at all. You have to respect her choice in this matter. All women have periods and it is a sign that her body is doing what it is supposed to and meant to do for procreation. Don't look at her period as dirty, nasty or gross. Her cycle is a part of life and is a necessary occurrence with all women of child bearing years.

The menstrual cycle usually begins after age 9 and before for age 16, typically between ages 11 and 14. The average cycle is 28 days, but can very from 24 to 35 days depending on the individual girl. These points are important because it explains how are bodies function and why.

TIME OUT: A WOMAN'S MENSTRUAL CYCLE

Day 1 -14 Beginning of Cycle
When the egg is not fertilized, estrogen and progesterone levels drop, and the thickened uterine lining is shed. The uterus sheds its blood-filled lining because it is not needed to support a fertilized egg. This portion of the cycle, called a PERIOD, usually lasts anywhere from three to seven days. In layman's terms, it is when she is bleeding.

Day 1	Day 2	Day 3	Day 4	Day 5	Day 6	Day 7
P	P	P	P	P	P	P
Day 8	Day 9	Day 10	Day 11	Day 12	Day 13	Day 14
						O
Day 15	Day 16	Day 17	Day 18	Day 19	Day 20	Day 21
Day 22	Day 23	Day 24	Day 25	Day 26	Day 27	Day 28
			PMS	PMS	PMS	PMS

About day 14 (Middle of Cycle) **OVULATION**
At the mid point of the cycle, in an ovary matures and an EGG is released into a fallopian tube where it travels down toward the uterus. As the egg moves down the fallopian tube:

> **THIS IS WHEN SHE OVULATES AND CAN GET PREGNANT.**

While the egg is present, any sperm that lives **72** hours before or after the egg arrives can be fertilized by the sperm. So if she has sex during that entire week and the man ejaculates inside her, his sperm can live for 3 whole days. The probability of her getting pregnant exists 3 days before and three days after her ovulation day. There is usually a week for this possibility.

That is why if a woman has sex with multiple men within 7-10 days of her ovulation, she can't be sure of whom the father is, and that is why the Maury Povich Show is so popular. Most women don't know as much about their own bodies as they should. As an extra measure, to avoid an unwanted pregnancy, restrain from intercourse during this time.

Days 14 through 28 (End of Cycle)
In response to follicle stimulating Hormone (FSH) being released from the pituitary gland in the brain, ultimately one EGG matures.

Pre-Menstrual Syndrome or otherwise known as PMS.
PMS is a woman's response to changing hormone levels. The symptoms are most intense in the 7 to 10 days before her period and they usually disappear a day or two after she starts.

Symptoms of PMS:

- ❖ Fluid retention (swollen fingers or ankles, puffy face)
- ❖ Bloating (feeling heavy, weight gain)
- ❖ Breast tenderness or swelling and moodiness (increased emotional sensitivity, crying, feeling depressed)
- ❖ Irritability (grouchy, impatience, quick to anger)
- ❖ Back pain or headache
- ❖ Diarrhea or constipation
- ❖ Skin problems or breakouts like Acne or rashes
- ❖ Food cravings (especially chocolate and other sweets or salty foods)
- ❖ Difficulty concentrating
- ❖ Fatigue and/or cramps
- ❖ Extreme lower back pain
- ❖ Extreme sexual desire or horniness

11 Things PMS Symptoms Could Stand For:

1. Pass My Shotgun
2. Psychotic Mood Shift
3. Perpetual Munching Spree
4. Puffy Mid-Section
5. People Make me Sick
6. Provide Me with Sweets
7. Pardon My Sobbing
8. Pimples May Surface
9. Pass My Sweat Pants
10. Pack My Shit
11. Potential Murder Suspect

If you had all the symptoms and changes happening to you and your body, you would be in a bad mood too. The good sign for you is that she may get extremely horny. This can happen while she is on or off her period. Some men shun the fact of having sex while she is bleeding. Others love it. If she takes a bath and is "fresh" she will not have an odor. (This preference is your own as long as you understand it isn't foul).

The key is to understanding PMS is looking out for the signs. Once you are with a woman for a while you will know when she is on her first day of her cycle, then three weeks from her first day is usually when PMS occurs. A man who pays attention will instinctively know when her mood uncharacteristically changes.

The best thing you can do if you notice she is not in a great mood is to offer to bring her chocolate, a heating pad and give her a back rub, then disappear. Not to worry, the symptoms do fade away within a few days and you will get your girl back.

CHAPTER 12

THE WARM-UP

We all like to be teased and tempted so as long as the gratification is within reach. Women need to be warmed up, not only to the idea of a sexual encounter, but the possibilities of what is to **come**.

FOREPLAY PHYSICAL VERSUS MENTAL

Foreplay with a woman starts long before you arrive in the bedroom. Men can have sex anytime, but most women need to be stimulated and prepared for sex. Massage her mind. Attention is great foreplay. **Let her know you crave her by the way you look at her, talk to her and what you do for her.** You may clean the house, or put oil in her car. You may grab her from behind and kiss her on her neck for no reason. You may turn off the TV and sit silently in a room together under the fireplace while reading. Mental foreplay can be a powerful aphrodisiac. Women appreciate the little things.

Make your side of the bed. Get up early to make her coffee. Call her at work and tell her you can't wait to see her. Wash the dishes if you have to. Small gestures, as I've said, go a long way. If you make her feel appreciated she will gladly return the favor. If she knows sex with her makes you happy, she will give you sex. But most men neglect the mental seduction aspect of the sex dance. So take the time to give her the ultimate warm-up: foreplay of the mind.

PHYSICAL

- Massage

What person says no to a sensual massage? Whether it is a full body massage at home, an invitation to share a couple's massage at a spa, or a foot rub after a night out on the town, no woman can say no to being pampered. Forget the magic stick; a man with a good touch can put a woman under his spell any day of the week. Lighting a scented candle or warming the oil gets you mad brownie points for the details. You can start with her neck or back, using proper massage oil. Firmly but gently knead her troubles away with long attentive strokes. If she moans or starts to breathe deeply you know she is relaxing. If you sense her tense up, ease up on your pressure. You can vary your strokes and hand positions to stimulate her blood flow in various directions. The right touch can make a woman excited and get her natural vaginal secretions flowing. Perfect for what you might have in mind next.

- Touching her

Can I get an amen for the men with the good hands? So many men rush to touch our breasts or our vagina that they forget our skin is the largest organ we have. Just imagine all the nerve endings that you pass over because you think her nipples and her sweet spot are the only body parts that you can touch to turn her on.

> **Women agree that a man that takes his time to explore our bodies with his hands, mouth, teeth and tongue make the best lovers.**

There are places on my body a man has never touched in a sensual way and those spots are perhaps the most sensitive. For example, my scalp just may be the most sensitive area on my body. I happen to be blessed and cursed with a head full of extraordinarily thick hair. A blessing, because it is versatile, and a curse, because the torture I go through to straighten it now. As a child, I'd cry for days at the thought of getting my hair combed. The old folks would say I'm "tender headed." The slightest tug at my hair would send me off crying and screaming. Now, less sensitive to the pain, my head seems to have billions of nerve endings. A proper head massage can excite me, turn me on, or even satisfy me. I'll leave the rest to your imagination. I don't even let strangers touch my head because it is so erotic. Not everyone can invade my personal space in that way. So make like William Shatner and go where no man has ever gone before with your woman.

Take your time. Run your fingers across the backs of her knees and the backs of her wrists, inner thighs, and waist. I can tell you what works on me but I have to keep something to myself. The idea here is to try to think *differently*. Instead of going straight to her nipples, try massaging and slowly touching the outside of her breasts and gently cupping them. Perhaps draw your tongue slowly across the bottom of them and create a circular motion then trace them from the outside to the middle. This is the time to be a tease. Don't be afraid to use your body to rub up against hers. Get behind her and press yourself against her luscious body while you play in her hair or stroke the bottom of her back. Reach deep into her V section without touching her vagina. I believe a woman can tell by the way a man touches her if he is "all man" and not someone posing on the 'down low'. Men who love women love every part of us. Women know when a man loves coochie. He shows it by the way he tastes her, touches her and experiences her body. He may just enjoy the experience more than she does. Make us know why you love us. Show us by what you do to us and how excited you can get while doing it. That is key. So, use your imagination and find the neglected nooks and crevices of our bodies with sensual touches or kisses. Let your fingers do the walking and don't forget to talk to her. Tell her the things you like while you are there. What a tease you are, you big flirt!

- Kinky Boots

Being a 'freak' in bed is relative. Everyone has their own definition of what a freak is. In Kansas, it might simply be leaving the lights on during sex. For others it might be the R. Kelley golden shower or a sexual act they may require a sheep, whipped cream, and a vacuum cleaner attachment. As long as you are not involving minors, what you do in your bedroom is your business. Men should always test the waters with their partners first before performing some outlandish, deviant, or wild sexual act. Most women like a little pulling of the hair, a little soft biting about her body, and gentle choking while stroking. The goal is not to hurt her—although some might argue no pain no pleasure—it is to turn her on in an animalistic way that excites her.

- Mutual masturbation

Two can play that game. After she is well relaxed and you are rubbing her body in a sensual way, you can easily move her to touch herself. This is often a good way to see how she likes to be touched. Show me and I'll show you. If you gently take her hand while she is in an uninhibited state, and slowly guide them along her body little by little and gently moving them around her V section, she might go into auto-pilot. A woman usually knows how to please herself just as a man does. Keep your hands on top of hers until she finds her spot. Once that occurs, you can slowly touch yourself. Motivating her by your sweet words like, "I love to see you touch yourself" can keep her going. She may become more motivated by seeing you so turned on by what she is doing to herself. Allow her to indulge while you do the same. This sensuous activity is a must exercise for all couples.

- Cunnilingus

Oral sex performed on a woman. It is fun to receive but giving is the ultimate pleasure. You asked, I'm telling. Most women, who don't have hang-ups about this, find oral sex to often be the most pleasurable foreplay. Usually, because most women can orgasm or the street word, "come," from stimulating her clitoris.

FLAG ON PLAY: Notice to the: "I don't like/ or never done it before" brothers out there...

Some of you brothers have a lot of hang-ups when it comes to 'going down'. You will claim that it doesn't smell right or you don't know how. You'll make any excuse to keep from doing right thing by her.

A healthy vagina has less germs and bacteria than the average person's mouth

The vagina, when healthy and free of infections and disease, naturally does not even need soap. It cleanses itself. A woman should not douche or use soap to clean herself because it destabilizes the natural pH balance and good bacteria she naturally has.

After a charity basketball game, I made the mistake of trying to explain this on a bus packed with men who proceeded to clown me the rest of the trip. I was merely pointing out a fact. I was not saying "I" never use soap. The type of cleansing agent I use is complementary to a woman's pH like Dove, although technically labeled a cleansing bar, not a soap, and has far less additives than regular soap and less chemical irritants. Needless to say, I became the brunt of every joke after that. I was nicknamed "stinky kitty", "poo poo puddy cat"—every childish joke that you can think of. It was quite a learning experience. At least I was among friends, and it was funny. I have always been able to laugh at myself.

But the information I tried dispensing is absolutely true. A woman should bathe in warm water and use soap around the area and for her pubic hair, but the vagina should only be cleansed externally with warm water or a pH friendly cleansing agent like Phisoderm, baby soap, or Dove—usually anything without perfumes or additives, or labeled for sensitive skin.

So this excuse is played. Every lady has a different scent, whether she smells like flowers or sweet potatoes. It should turn you on because it is unique to her. So stop making excuses! There is a first time for everything. And if she is into it, I know she will help you master the art with little resistance.

So now you are hungry and want to "eat," what do we like and how do we like it?

HOW TO GIVE PROPER HEAD

Okay, you got me. This is not my area of expertise. I have never performed oral sex on a woman, and I've never had a woman perform oral sex on me. But enough about me already! Being a good lover is part technique and part willingness to learn what you need to do to turn your girl on. It is impossible to know everything. But the openness to learn is often the biggest turn on. Giving great head is an art no doubt. You don't want to be that brother that gets "the tap" on the shoulder after you thought you were putting it down. Rather, you want to be that resourceful guy who is willing to go the extra mile to make her smile or scream. Even if you fall short of perfection, we will love you for the effort and passion behind the attempt.

Talk to her, ask her what she likes and pay attention to her breathing and body language. With women, this is the cardinal rule. If you are trying something new, an attentive lover will pick up on all the crucial clues.

I suggest taking notes and reading one of my favorite books on this subject, *How To Give Her Absolute Pleasure* written by Lou Paget who has been featured on HBO's Great Sex series. I found this book to be most on point in this area. This book is definitely for the men who want to be "King of Head in Bed," so run out and study up!

HOW TO GET A WOMAN TO DO WHATEVER YOU WANT

Now that you have the basic steps in giving her what she wants, she will be remiss not to give you want you want. This only happens if you have done so out of selflessness and a genuine desire to please her. Getting a woman to be your willing love slave is fairly simple. We are hungry for positive attention and for love. We want to believe in romance and that 'the one' will arrive on a flying horse, scoop us up, propose to us, pay our bills, and carry us off to live in his mansion on the top of the Eiffel tower. Babyface is partially to blame for this nonsense!

A woman must feel safe. Safety for her means that she can trust you. It also means she is assured that you won't embarrass her and that she can open herself up to new ideas without negative repercussions. You never know what level of freak a woman has in her. If you make her comfortable from the onset by treating her like a queen, and if you boost her ego and confidence she will be willing to do whatever it takes to make you happy *within* her comfort level.

HARD CORE OR ROUGH SEX PRECAUTION

Caution to the rough sex players out there: If it ever gets too heated in bed, I suggest having a safety word. This is a word that when you hear it you both stop. Like PURPLE or MULHOLLAND. A word that is distinguishable so each of you immediately recognizes it and immediately stops. That way, you establish the rules up front. It's always good to talk about what is about to go down. It can ruin the spontaneity of the mood but it manages expectations. Have a safety word so things don't get out of control.

NO MEANS NO!

Never take advantage of an inebriated woman. Just because she cannot say no, does not mean she is saying yes. Not being able to say no does not constitute an implied consent.

If you find yourself with a woman who is totally wasted, the gentlemanly thing to do, is to take her home and put her to bed. Sleep on a couch if you must spend the night. Further, **if you hear a woman say no at <u>any</u> point during sex, even if you have entered her, you must immediately stop.** It is not the most romantic situation and definitely one of the most frustrating for a man. But stopping will keep you out of jail. It's better for her to say stop, than you saying stop to your new 6'6", 350 pound cellmate!

CHAPTER 13

FULL COURT PRESS

Relationships are based on what you put into them. You get what you are willing to give. You should constantly desire to evolve and make yourself a better person in a relationship and in life. As you grow, the relationship should grow. But sometimes, that growth may mean that the two of you have grown apart as you each realize that your needs have changed in the past two, three, or five years.

You have to be fair in a relationship, and respect the fact that you can be different but also exist in harmony with your own unique set of beats. Setting the tone of the relationship from the beginning is crucial. The rules are established up front. If you allow yourself to be at her beck and call and allow yourself to be treated in any kind of way, then that's what she will always expect of you. If you veer from this, the relationship may deteriorate. Stay on your toes.

- Stay interesting
- Keep sex fun

Don't be predictable.

Be consistent; just don't be predictable. Boring is bad. Coming home every night and vegging out in front of the TV is boring. Being consistent means you usually have an even personality which is predictable in a great way that women love. Women love a constant, a "fixed rate" man if you will. No one wants to deal with someone with violent mood swings. Keep the variables at a minimum. Being someone who is there for her is the über sexy. There is no bigger turn on. Women need consistency and stability. Having a man who is her rock—there is nothing better.

GIVE EACH OTHER SPACE

Never try to change someone. Sometimes we fall in love with our partner's potential instead of the reality of who that person really is. Part of love is supporting each other to become their best. Having someone who brings out the best in you is the best-case scenario. Together you can be a positive force in each other's lives. Like the movie says, "You make me want to be a better man," Now, where are my tissues and my damn chocolate?!

Also, the happiest couples give each other breathing room. Having your own friendships and your own hobbies strengthens the relationship because you always have something new and interesting to share.

MANAGE YOUR PRIVACY
In the 21st century, communication is highly evolved.

147

Technology has evolved. There is e-mail, instant messaging, MMS, picture sharing, camera phones, instant credit reports, instant online background checks, national sexual offender databases, reverse phone number and address books, property searches, navigation systems, video phones, car location, speed monitoring, logs for locations and time, identity theft, and privacy issues. The Internet is as much evil as it is good. You can run but you can no longer hide.

In the beginning, it is always best to manage your privacy by safeguarding your belongings also. Don't leave your credit cards, checkbooks, jewelry, Blackberrys, or personal banking information lying around until you fully trust the woman you are dating. Limit what strangers or new friends have access to. This is just common sense. Know whom you have in your circle of trust at first.

By the same token, keep voicemail, passwords, and log in information locked away. Do not use the same number for everything. If you have a stalker/snooper on your hands and she figures out the code to your voicemail on your cell phone, she will now have access to your work voicemail, pager, all of your e-mail addresses and so on. It is also advisable that you change them once a month.

This also applies to giving your house key to someone. Keep in mind most keys can be copied. You don't want to come home one day after you break up with someone and find your beloved pet rabbit boiling on the stove. I cannot stress these points enough.

KEEPING IT REAL
- Do not do things or say things because you believe that is what she wants or what she wants to hear.
- Be honest about the relationship.

DO NOT TELL A WOMAN YOU LOVE HER IF YOU DON'T

Don't let her think it's going to be serious if it is just a fling. If you are just having fun and not ready to be tied down or not ready to be in a relationship, or in a relationship with her, simply, say so. You don't want her out shopping for wedding dresses in her spare time.

Women fall in love faster than men. Even if she tells you she loves you first, does not obligate you to say it to her in return. Do not allow her to guilt you into saying it back to her. If you are guilty of saying you love someone because they told you first, you are probably a kind person. But this is lying. It is difficult when you care for a woman to hurt her feelings. But the truth is, better to break it to her sooner than later. Later, she will be **more** emotionally invested. If she thinks you love her, she will have a greater expectation of the relationship. This "emotional deceit" on your part inevitably inflicts more pain than is necessary. Let her deal with the let down in her own time. Do not make it worse by living a lie.

By the same token, if you are in a relationship and want to know if a woman really loves you, as a rule, look to what she *shows* you, not what she *says*. Anyone with a tongue can tell us they love us. But what do they show us? Ask yourself these questions: Is she thoughtful? Is she kind? Is she there when I need her? Is she there for me emotionally, physically, spiritually and any other way imaginable? Is she attentive? Does she reciprocate? Does she make me feel emotionally safe? These are indications of how much we mean to them. We don't always need the words. We need to see the words in **action**. Show me you love me. Show me how you feel about me. Words are cheap. Unequivocally, it is best to show someone how you feel through your actions.

ARGUMENTS/ FIGHTING FAIR

No one likes to talk about difficult issues. This communication should be second nature if we were raised in an environment where our families were capable of honest, loving and open communication. But let's face the facts. **None of us lived on the Cosby Show.** Most of our families avoided negative feelings at all costs. Anything that disrupted the appearance of harmony was something we hid. We swallowed our emotions. In the more dysfunctional families, loving communication might have been acting out or rationalizing negative feelings. We reprimanded our children by yelling, or through spankings, beatings (whippings) or verbal abuse. The "you are so stupid, you'll never be anything, I can't stand you" statements are examples of verbal abuse. The Christian Bible says: spare the rod, spoil the child. But the issue of to beat or not to beat is a whole other book. My point being, the goal was supposed to be to teach children right from wrong.

If our models showed us how to effectively and lovingly communicate, without suppressing negative feelings or through abusive measures we were encouraged and felt safe to discover and explore our own negative reactions and feelings through trial and error. Through positive role models we would have learned successfully how to communicate even our most difficult feelings. Throughout our formative years, childhood, adolescence, and throughout young adulthood, we would have gradually learned to express our feelings respectfully and appropriately and freely. The bottom line is, most of us did not have this positive familial structure growing up.

When it comes to fighting or disagreements, unfortunately, there are very few people who can express themselves when they are angry in a constructive and truthful manner to resolve issues. We want to lash out because <u>anger is a form of pain</u>.

You are angry that someone you care about and trust hurt you.

We become reactionary. We speak without thinking and instantly react to our emotions. We do this because we are imperfect. Somehow, we never developed the tools to handle our anger and disappointments.

In order to avoid fighting while angry and creating a snowball effect making matters worse or saying unforgivable things, try to use these tools:

TOOLS FOR FIGHTING FAIR

- Don't harbor negative feelings.
- Bring issues up when you are not upset.
- Never fight when you are angry.
- Cool off first, tell her you are angry and you need some time to think.
- Take the time to write down what you are really upset about.
- Go work out, play basketball, or hang with your friends to relax and take your mind off the situation for the moment.

When you do speak to your partner, ask them to listen to you without interrupting until are done. You are letting her know that she will have the opportunity to respond, but you will not continue if she does not respect what you have to say.

Here is a guideline of how you might approach the conversation:

- Be specific
- Be honest
- Be focused
- Use a cheat sheet or talking points if you have to

I find it constructive to have some standard sentences I can use to help me figure out what I am trying to say or even determine why I am upset or hurt to begin with. You can use the following to start off sentences and to help you formulate your thoughts in a constructive manner:

1. When you did or you said _____.
2. I felt _____.
3. It hurt me because _____.
4. I may have _____.
5. I know you probably did not mean to hurt me or make me feel like _____.
6. If this ever happens again_____. Or
7. To avoid this from happening again_____.

DEALING WITH A VIOLENT WOMAN
As much as you try to keep a situation from getting out of hand, sometimes the woman you are involved with can't control her anger without hitting of throwing things at you.

But being a man, you are held to a higher expectation of physical restraint. With that said, you can never hit a woman.

NEVER EVER HIT A WOMAN

Walk away or end the relationship, if necessary, if you feel even the remote possibility of violence on your part. Violence and abuse includes choking, slapping, grabbing, or any and all forms of **intimidation.** Sometimes, our anger can get the best of us. Even the most even-tempered people can be pushed too far. If all else fails and you no longer feel that you can control your actions, GET OUT!

➢ She provoked you.
➢ She made you hit her.
➢ She deserved to be hit.
➢ You can't stop yourself from hitting a woman.
➢ You can't help yourself.
➢ She was asking for it.

None of these are ever valid reasons for striking someone.

If you find yourself in a volatile argument with someone, tell them in an authoritative, matter-of-fact manner, that if they don't calm down, you will, leave. If she persists, you must do exactly what you have warned, LEAVE. If this happens more than once and she finds herself alone and irate, she will eventually get the point. You must teach people how to treat you. You are teaching her that if she does not control her anger and continues to disrespect you, you will either leave the room or you will

153

leave the house until she calms down. After a day or two of not hearing from you, she may have thought about what she said or the way she overreacted and become more pliable. Let's hope that by then, she'll have found a better way to express herself.

- NEVER HIT BELOW THE BELT

There should always be boundaries and lines you do not cross even when you are furious with someone. *How* you fight is usually the number one factor in determining if a couple will remain together or not. There is a level of respect that you should have for your partner even when you are angry. Once something is said, you can't magically take it back. The damage is done and those hurt feelings will be memorialized. There are things you should never say to each other when upset. **Once you have chopped a man's balls off, you cannot sew them back on.** Once you have deeply, emotionally injured a woman, she may never forget or forgive you.

For instance, if a woman is extremely upset with a man she should never say, "That's why your penis is so small". Comments like these are never constructive and only tear down the very fiber of a man. He needs to be respected. If a woman says things to you like that let her go, she is not worth it. The relationship has deteriorated to a level of no return. Sometimes people do not know how to correctly express themselves without being hurtful. If a woman can, or man for that matter, try to strike back by tearing down one's self-esteem in or out of anger, that person does not deserve to be in relationship with you.

154

THE NATIONAL ANGER MANAGEMENT ASSOCIATION is a good place to start to seek help if you believe you have a problem controlling your anger.

Contact Information:
National Anger Management Association (NAMA)
Telephone (646)-485-5116 Fax (646) 390-1571
NAMA, PO Box 20993, Park West Station, New York, NY 10025 Email - namass@namass.org

BREAKING UP

Breaking up is never easy but it is absolutely necessary. When it isn't working, and you have tried, and tried, and you realize, you want to break up, take the time to plan. Maybe you need time, maybe you need space, maybe you just aren't sure of your feelings anymore. Whatever the case, if you decide to break up with someone, do these things:

GIVE HER CLOSURE

Closure. You have heard this word and probably don't fully understand what it means. It simply means in man speak, "tell her you are breaking up with her and why so she can move on with her life." When a woman is in love or has ever cared for a man she has been in a relationship with, we sometimes can't move on when you abruptly disappear. While you may think that is a proper and acceptable way to break things off, let me be crystal, it is not. By becoming distant or completely disappearing, she could think you will come back one day. What is cruel is when a man never says anything and just stops calling her or communicating with her altogether. No one deserves this type of treatment. Not even a mangy dog on the street.

Three words. **BE - A - MAN.** If you care anything at all for that woman, whether it is just a basic friendship, broken engagement, or short-term relationship, the mark of a real man is to face his responsibility and do what he has to do even though it may be difficult. When you are honest with a woman whether she wants to hear what you have to say or not, you'll always end up, in time, with a friend. You never want to be labeled as "that guy who messed it up for every other guy to come along after you." Or when she speaks of you she has very choice words like asshole, M.F., B@tch ass n#gga..., I'm sure you can fill in the rest of the blanks. You never want to have anyone feel this way about you if you are truly a good person.

There is nothing better for a woman than to walk away from her relationship with her dignity in tact. She still has opportunities to connect with someone else on a deeper level, and perhaps that someone is out there waiting for her. By giving her closure, you leave her with hope and promise, as opposed to hatred and her plotting how she will break into your house and spray paint obscenities across the walls. Or worse, when she sees you out, it's open season to clown you with your new friends, dates, or God forbid, your new girlfriend.

Your explanation could be as simple as, "It's just not working." It does not have to be a laundry list of everything you believe is wrong with her or wrong in the relationship. It should be as kind as possible without lying. You do not have to say you have met someone else if you have. All you have to say is, "It's not you it's me," which still could apply if she turns out to be a psycho, because you realized she was crazy as hell! That particular break-up "line" is becoming more cliché than anything, but is still the gold standard of break-up explanations.

If it is too difficult for you to say in person, send a letter or e-mail or call her. But it has to be *done*. Of course, it is more personal to do it face to face, but if you find it impossible or are just plain scared she may try to harm you, then by all means, send a letter or fax if you have to. But do or convey **something**.

Also, a lot of men get intimidated when things get too close too soon as I stated earlier. If this applies to your situation, you can offer her this, "I'm not ready and I don't want to hurt you anymore than I already have." Yes, she will be hurt but there can be an end to her pain. These are very *kind* words and she will be able to walk away knowing that she was with a good man. She was with a man who was honest with her and respected her at the end of the day.

The key thing is that she will be able to move on with her life. You do not want to hinder her ability to heal or be the one responsible for emotional scars she may carry in her heart.

Be gentle with us because one day, if not now, you will have a daughter or sister or mother and you would not want to see any of those women that are so dear to you hurt in an unnecessary way.

Now, on the other hand, if you tell her you are breaking up with her and she refuses to believe you, and chooses to live a fairy tale life with you in her mind and believe that you will be back, then the responsibility is all on her. But I warn you…

> **DO NOT HAVE SEX WITH HER AFTER YOU END THE RELATIONSHIP. IF YOU DO, AND YOU HAVE NO INTENTION ON GETTING BACK TOGETHER, YOU ARE PLAYING WITH FIRE!**

If you insist on doing this, you are asking for trouble. You are sending mixed messages by making love to her. You are playing with her emotions and that is a dangerous game. This means baby's mamas, ex-wives, and ex-girlfriends. Don't do it. You've been warned.

Break up and break up clean. When you do, know you have done the right thing. The kind thing. The courageous and responsible thing.

CHAPTER 14

GAME RULES REPLAY

So you think you've got game? Now go and get that girl! Just remember to apply all the rules from the previous chapters and you will be the MVP.

1. Never ever lie to a woman. Honesty is the ultimate aphrodisiac.
2. Never ever hit a woman.
3. Always project confidence.
4. Never invalidate a woman's feelings.
5. Learn to listen.
6. Never feel intimidated by a woman. All women are attainable.
7. Don't try to change her feelings when she is upset.
8. Get to know the woman you are interested in.
9. Be her genuine friend.
10. Always encourage a woman's dreams and aspirations.
11. Never date or pursue married women.
12. Never treat all women the same. All women are not created equal.
13. Respect her if she deserves respect.
14. Always be honest about the relationship.
15. Always be tactful.
16. Always be prepared for dates.
17. Never hate on other men.
18. Never brag about your sexual prowess or penis size.

19. Never name drop about celebrity friends.
20. Encourage her at all times to be who she really is.
21. Never lead a woman to believe the relationship is more than it is.
22. Do not do things or say things because you believe that is what she wants or what she wants to hear.
23. Give her closure if you break up.
24. Do not tell a woman you love her if you do not.
25. Never tell a woman she would look good pregnant if you do not want a baby with her.
26. Don't discuss marriage in detail if you do not have those thoughts about her.
27. Do not have unprotected sex if you do not want a child with the woman you are sleeping with.
28. If you plan on having sex with someone, get tested together first.
29. Fight Fair. Never hit below the belt.
30. Don't grab a woman by the arm when trying to get her attention.
31. Don't talk too close or invade her personal space.
32. Always read a woman's body language.
33. Do not use your friend to approach a woman for you.
34. Don't get too familiar too soon by giving us nicknames and such.
35. Do not use corny pick up lines unless they are meant to be corny.
36. Do not pull along side us while driving and ask us to come over.
37. Do not make overtly sexual comments to us.
38. Do not approach a woman who gives you all the signs that she is not interested.
39. Do use the preferred approach methods in Chapter 6.

40. Always be willing to walk away.
41. Never call a woman as soon as you get her phone number.
42. Always give a woman your e-mail address or business card and ask for hers.
43. Don't call a woman more than twice without getting a return call.
44. Do show her you are interested in her.
45. Don't send multiple unanswered e-mails or text messages.
46. Don't have more than three conversations with her before asking her out.
47. Allow her to get to know you.
48. Let her go at her own pace where she is always comfortable.
49. Never pressure her for sex.
50. Don't reveal your problems or issues too early in the relationship.
51. Don't talk about other people in a negative way.
52. Always be a source of inspiration and support in her life.
53. Never complain about anything that you don't like about her.
54. Turn your cell off while you're out with her.
55. Put in the work. Know the type of woman you are dealing with or desire to know better.
56. Don't Google her or ask everyone in town about her.
57. Don't try to make the first move on the first 3 dates.
58. Never expect sex.
59. Do not place a time limit on sex.
60. Never try to talk a woman into having sex with you.
61. Do not try to seduce an inebriated woman.

62. Do not intentionally withhold compliments because you think she hears them all the time.
63. Don't flirt with her friends or pay too much attention to them.
64. Make your dates fun and interesting.
65. Never forget her birthday.
66. Never forget Valentine's Day.
67. Always give her romantic gifts for romantic occasions.
68. Stay out of the "friends" category.
69. Don't be a "Mark" AKA a sucker.
70. Don't be shy or bashful, always project confidence.
71. Don't laugh too much on a date for no reason or be silly or talk too much.
72. Dress appropriately on dates.
73. Don't be corny.
74. Go places she wants to go.
75. Be affectionate toward her.
76. Don't show signs of weakness.
77. Take control if the situation allows.
78. Never bluntly criticize a woman or tell her what you do NOT like about her or degrade her in any way.
79. Always have safe sex by using a latex condom and always check the expiration date.
80. Tell a woman your HIV status and if you have any diseases that can be transmitted to her.
81. Never depend on a woman to provide contraception.
82. No one position or move/method works on all women.
83. Get to know what she likes in bed. Ask her.
84. Make no subject off limits.
85. Tell her what you like in subtle ways.

86. Tell her what you think is attractive about her personality.
87. Don't be too proud to learn what pleases her.
88. Never assume she is satisfied because you think she had an orgasm during sex.
89. Never be afraid to talk during sex.
90. Always be open to listening and learning in relationships.
91. Never be afraid to try new things.
92. Don't discuss your sex life with your friends.
93. Be aware of a woman's insecurities about her body image. Never say anything to point out a flaw on her body.
94. Know a woman's menstrual cycle and learn to look for the signs of PMS.
95. Do engage in foreplay.
96. Stay interesting.
97. Keep sex fun and fresh.
98. Manage your privacy.
99. Always talk when you are not angry after a fight or misunderstanding.
100. NEVER RUN AWAY FROM A GREAT WOMAN.

To all the men who have taken time to read this book, I thank you. You have the desire to be the best man you can be and the willingness to treat yourself and all women you may pursue with the respect they deserve.

At the end of the day, if you follow these basic rules and guidelines, whether you get the woman of your dreams or not, she will be missing out on a great man who is willing to be the best man he can possibly be for himself, and any lady who happens to have the pleasure of getting to know him.

Having *Game* is having technique **without** playing games. It is getting to know a woman without lies and without deceit. You must be yourself from day one. She must not be led to believe you are one person the first day you meet, and six months later find out you are someone else. If you do this, you were being "fake" because you presented who you thought she would want you to be. You surmised that it would be easier to get her in bed by doing so. Wrong!

Just be you! Do you! If she is not interested in the real you, then keep it moving because someone else will.

-Mizz Moore

ABOUT THE AUTHOR

Former Model and Detroit native Kenya Moore is perhaps most recognized for being crowned Miss USA, making her the second African-American to be bestowed with such a prestigious honor. She has since become a popular actress starring on numerous television shows such as *Girlfriends*, *Martin*, and *The Steve Harvey Show* just to name a few. She has also starred in feature films which include *"Deliver Us From Eva"*, *"Waiting to Exhale"*, and independent blockbuster *"Trois."* Moore can also be seen opposite Lindsay Lohan in her latest movie, *"I Know Who Killed Me"* released in late July. She earned a magna cum laude GPA from Wayne State University in psychology with a minor in communications. Adding the title Producer and Writer to her list of talents, **GAME, GET SOME!** is Kenya's first literary work.

Visit KENYAMOORE.COM or MySpace.com/KENYAMOORE for more info about Kenya.

Printed in the United States
89767LV00003B/166-306/A